W9-BKM-240

Presented to

_____

By

_____

_____

date

POWER IDEAS
for
A HAPPY FAMILY

Robert H. Schuller

Fleming H. Revell Company
Old Tappan, New Jersey

Unless otherwise identified, Scripture quotations are from the
Revised Standard Version of the Bible, Copyrighted 1946 and 1952.
Scripture quotations identified LB are from *The Living Bible*
by Kenneth N. Taylor, copyright © 1971 and are used by permission of the publisher, Tyndale House Publishers.

Grateful acknowledgment is hereby made for quotations from
the following publications:

Marriage Lines by Ogden Nash ("A Word to Husbands"), published by Little, Brown and Company. Copyright © 1912 by
Ogden Nash. Used by permission.

Letters to Karen by Charlie W. Shedd, published by Abingdon
Press. Used by permission.

Easy to Live With by Leslie Parrott. Beacon Hill Press of
Kansas City. Used by permission.

Virginia Graham's Advice to Wives by Muriel Davidson. Reprinted by permission of the William Morris Agency on behalf
of Muriel Davidson. Copyright © 1971 by The Hearst Corporation.

Letters to Philip by Charlie W. Shedd. Copyright © 1968 by
Charlie W. Shedd and the Abundance Foundation. Reprinted by
permission of Doubleday & Company, Inc.

Love Poems for the Very Married by Lois Wyse. Copyright ©
1970 by Lois Wyse. Reprinted by permission of The World Pub-
lishing Company, New York, N.Y.

This volume is a revision of POWER IDEAS FOR SUCCESSFUL
FAMILIES, copyright © 1971 by Robert Harold Schuller, and
material from that work is used by permission of the author.

ISBN 0 8007 0525 4
Copyright © 1972 by Robert Harold Schuller
Published by the Fleming H. Revell Company
All Rights Reserved
Library of Congress Catalog Card Number: 79-186539
Printed in the United States of America

TO the thousands of happy families in Garden Grove Community Church who are a constant source of inspiration to me.

CONTENTS

INTRODUCTION

If you and your family are enjoying happiness and health, then you will share my enthusiasm in this book. Read on and cheer for the American home!

If you and your family are struggling to survive pressures that threaten to disintegrate your marriage and family, then you can find the secret of success in these pages. I have counseled with thousands of married couples and parents and know that IMPOSSIBLE SITUATIONS CAN BECOME POSSIBLE MIRACLES THROUGH POSSIBILITY THINKING!

Begin *now* by believing in the exciting, fruitful, joyous future of the time-tested institutions of marriage and the family.

Good news! The experts, who have been predicting the demise of these institutions, are wrong! The family is here to stay. Recently I heard Margaret Meade say, "All attempts in human history to eradicate the family have failed. The family will change form and life-style —but it is here to stay."

Of course, the negative thinkers who are trying to label the family as an obsolete, unworkable establishment are frequently speaking from a prejudiced platform. Take the Marxists, for example. Slyly, subtly, without revealing their communist beliefs, they write and speak their sophisticated theories about the death of the family. They insist that our society needs a revolution and will have one. What we need is a *revivolution*—not *revolution!*

We must revive faith in the family with all its infinite possibilities for joy, laughter, love, concern, compassion, courage and faith.

Consider, too, the prejudiced homosexuals who are conspiring against the family. I recently read a devastating, negative article on marriage and the family— written by an outspoken, antiheterosexual human being. Fairness demands that such persons disqualify themselves as jurors by reason of negative prejudice.

Then there are the losers who are trying to lead the way. In not a few instances the antifamily, anti-marriage voices are themselves the emotionally distorted products of a broken family. They simply never experienced joyous family life as children. When they married, they carried their faulty childhood examples of parenthood into their own marriage, which was, consequently, doomed at the outset. Now, armed with a college degree and a lifetime of tragic, negative, destructive memories, they dare to speak out in cynical sentences. In fairness, they should admit that their experiences may be limiting their creativity.

I believe in the family because I am the happy product of a happy family. I am the youngest of five children, born to an Iowa farming family. My parents laughed, loved, and fought, but stuck together through thick and thin, growing richer in character during their fifty-five years of marriage which was finally terminated by death. I am married to my first and only wife. We have five children, all planned, and our marriage and home are healthy and strong in spite of the fact that we live a high-pressure life in a fast-paced Southern California society.

Join me, then, in the greatest of all social adventures and challenges—making your family a fun-filled place of happy excitement!

POWER IDEAS
for
A HAPPY FAMILY

1
_____

THE FAMILY

The Greatest Institution in the World

What is a family?

It is the smallest unit of society. Planet earth is made up of continents, made up of nations, made up of states, made up of communities, and made up of families.

The family is a little town, a tiny state, a mini-nation. In government, more often than not, the family is more of an autocracy than a democracy.

The husband is a King.
The wife is a Queen.
Every son is a Prince.
Every daughter is a Princess.

At best, this form is a benevolent autocracy. The king holds court from time to time to confer what is best for all his subjects. His great heart beats with love for all his loyal and loving countrymen.

Here is a government where every citizen has a hot line to the head of state. The family is the one institution where any member can reach the top man at anytime. I recall how impressed I was one day when I was with Dr. Norman Vincent Peale in his private study in New York. It was several years ago when his book *The Power of Positive Thinking* was on the bestseller list. We were in a deep and earnest conversation when his secretary interrupted us, saying, "Excuse me, Dr. Peale, but Elizabeth is on the line."

"Oh, yes," he said, leaping from a relaxed pose in his old chair and energetically jumping to catch the phone. "Yes, Liz. How are you?" His face showed deep concern. The telephone conversation lasted for nearly fifteen minutes. Occasionally he would look my way, smile or wave, to assure me he would be back with me. But all his attention was focused on his teen-aged daughter at the other end of the line. He listened. He murmured a word or two from time to time. His silence was most impressive. To me it said, "Here's one of the greatest men of our time whose first love is his family." Finally he spoke into the telephone. She had obviously poured her heart out and it was his turn to respond. "Now, Lizabeth, don't you worry. So you didn't win the election—that's no disgrace to the Peales. I know you conducted a clean, Christian campaign. This is your chance to show everyone you know how to be a good loser! Your mother and I are proud of you, Liz. You're beautiful. We love you. You're the greatest." As he said it, I thought I saw a bright and beautiful glisten come across the gentle, wise eyes of my hero, Dr. Peale.

So, when from the Schuller home we sent our oldest

child off to an Eastern college, I said to her, "Remember your name—Sheila Schuller. Live up to it. Bring glory and honor to it. Let no conduct on your part bring shame to this name. In return, know that you can call anytime, and our hearts will leap to your heart; our dreams and projects will fade away and all of our hopes will rush to meet your hopes when you call to us. Single, or married, you will always have a special open line to the desk of the president of the little nation in which you will always enjoy full citizenship privileges as long as you shall live."

As a mini-nation the family has a unique diplomatic corps. In this, the smallest of all countries, every member from child to adult, is an ambassador-at-large. Every member, young or old, is made to feel that as he moves in other countries, cities, circles, or communities, outside his family borders, he is an ambassador for his family. From childhood he is taught, rightly, to be at his best behavior while away from home, or in the company of others outside his family circle.

When our oldest daughter, away from home, had to make a social decision that she felt could have proven a possible embarrassment to her family, she called us, checked and explained. This was more than we could expect from the younger children who, because of their youth, sometimes do embarrass the family a little. It reminds me of the time our son Robert was sitting in the car with a visiting guest from the east, Dr. Howard Hagaman. I was driving and ran out of gas. I left my five-year-old son in the car with Dr. Hagaman while I walked to the nearest gas station. While I was gone the good guest reached in his pocket and pulled out a cigarette. My son was shocked. I had been brainwashing his young mind against cigarettes only a few days before, telling him, "If you smoke cigarettes you'll get cancer."

"What's that?" he had asked.

I replied, "Well, just remember it's the worst disease you can possibly imagine." I dropped it at that. Now my son looked with frightened eyes at the smoke that was coming out of that face, leaking out of the nose and mouth of this human being. Very undiplomatically the young ambassador of the Schuller family said, "Oh, you mustn't do that or you'll get a terrible disease."

The very dignified doctor said, "Oh, really! And what might that be?"

And the little prince replied (after a long, thoughtful pause), "Diarrhea!"

As a tiny nation the family has a most unique economic system. A voluntary sharing of money is the quick and natural thing to do whenever a financial crisis arises. Here a sick child can receive unlimited and unrecorded welfare without embarrassment. The king will sell the land he owns, and risk walking the streets in rags if necessary, to raise the money to save the life, health and welfare of one of his beloved children.

MENTAL HEALTH CENTER

Psychologists are frustrated today. Why do we have this growing mental problem in our nation? What's the cause of it? And what's the solution?

One of the creative solutions is small-group therapy. This approach says that what people need is an opportunity to get in a small group where they can open themselves up; where they can express their inner fears, insecurities and inadequacies; where they can be honest and bare their fearful and guilty souls to a few loving friends, and where they can make confession of what they have done that is wrong and know that they will be forgiven.

This is what is needed—small therapeutic groups where you can expose your soul, where people in turn can be honest and blunt with you, and tell you honestly what no one dares to tell you! Still, there must be a dimension of affection that assures the worst member that he will never be abandoned and rejected. He will be accepted even if he is seen at his worst.

Why do we need small groups? What we are trying to do is create families. A family is the original small, sharing group. Because the family is falling down on the job, we are trying to create other so-called little families in our community.

What is a family? A family is a place where a few people—two, three, four or more—form a caring, sharing, bearing, baring, daring, small therapeutic fellowship. In this small group the members are blunt, at times almost cruel with each other; still, they love each other deeply. What other kind of social structure is there where you can tell people right to their faces what you think and know, in a loving relationship for the purpose of helping each other? Move out into the larger social group and people are not honest with you. We're all smart enough to be diplomatic. We're all taught to be tactful. We practice the simple rules of how to make friends and influence people. We have to. There are many immature people who are so touchy and sensitive that you couldn't be honest with them. They'd get mad and quit, and you'd never see them again.

Why is it that people grow up and have all kinds of mental conflicts? <u>A lot of our mental illness in America occurs in people who have never learned to take criticism and accept discipline, because they grew up in families where there was a lack of discipline.</u> When they get out into the brutal, hard-hitting, tough world, they can't take it. As children, they heard their parents fight or quarrel and saw them escape in easy divorce. So the emerging child learned a losing lesson: When faced with a problem—run! For this reason, many once-divorced parents remarry and stay married the second time. There are still arguments, but in this wiser-from-experience family there is a demonstration of deep, group commitment.

The family is a group that you know will take you in when you come back knocking at the door, and you know they will still love you even when they have heard and seen you at your worst.

Here is the one group that will take you in when the whole world shuts you out.

Here is the one circle of persons who will care enough to cry over your hurts when no one else gives a thought about you.

IMPROVING YOUR FAMILY

How can you make your family the greatest institution in the world?

1. Commit yourself with total dedication to the goal of making your family strong, loving, and beautiful.

Success comes when you set a goal and make that goal the most important thing in your life.

If with all your heart you want more than anything else in the world to make your family great, you *will* make it great.

2. Follow winners—don't follow losers.

Listen to those who have succeeded and are succeeding. Don't listen to the failures. Let a winner lead the way! Don't listen to the negative advice of people who have failed. Listen to the award winners and let the champions inspire you. There are millions of families that are strong and solid fortresses of faith, hope and love. Listen to people like Dr. Norman and Mrs.

Ruth Peale, or Dr. Billy and Mrs. Ruth Graham. You
will find that, with rare exception, the winning families
are families that read the Bible, pray, and practice a
vital religion. Successful homes are imbued with the
Spirit of God.

3. Form and frame a reasonable set of expectations.

Don't expect your family to be heaven on earth.
Don't expect perpetual peace and harmony. Expect
conflict; it doesn't mean your family is sick—it is a
sign that you are all growing. This is a sign of growth
and a symbol of change.

In *Easy to Live With,* Dr. Leslie Parrott writes a
call and challenge for readjustment.

> There is no such thing as an "ideal" home in
> which everything runs smoothly, where there are
> no cross words or where problems never arise.
> If there is a home like that, somebody is hiding
> something.
>
> Then, many people forget that one main func-
> tion of the family is to provide a setting where
> they may let down, release the safety valve, and
> let off tensions which have been building during
> a day at school or work. If the relationships in
> the home are so fragile that an honest expression
> of tension-releasing behavior cannot be absorbed,
> then the family foundation is faulty. The home
> is a place where we may express ourselves hon-
> estly without fear of retaliation because we know

  and understand each other in love.

Also, many people forget that living close together over long periods of time can be very exasperating. One of the men on the first expedition of Admiral Byrd to the South Pole told of the difficult circumstances of having a dozen men living together in exceedingly close quarters for the winter's night which lasted six months. They learned each other's idiosyncrasies. They learned how the other fellows tied their shoelaces, cleared their throats, or hummed an old tune. They learned to know each other so well that their close quarters drove them to the brink of despair and madness. In later years the bonds of friendship were lasting and fulfilling, but during the long months of living very close together the men were irritable and constantly exasperated with each other.

4. Dare and decide to make your family morally distinctive.

Mexico has different laws from Canada. Our family has some rules that make us different from other families on our block. For instance, we have always had the rule forbidding our children to play with the children on our street on Sunday. This one day in the week is confined to family and church influence only. We have strict rules on television. No shows depicting violence are allowed. Does the program inspire, amuse, or uplift? If not, it is at best a waste of time and, at worst, a destructive influence. We do not permit loud, harsh music in our home. We sense, in our home at least, that it generates vibrations which are not conducive to tranquil emotional health.

5. Learn to ask big questions.

When conflict arises, as it will every few months, don't lapse into impossibility thinking: "I've had it. It's no use. I'm getting out."

Neither do you point fingers, accuse or condemn. Rather you ask *big questions*. Dr. Robert Merkel, head of the counseling center in our church said, "Every problem we see here is the result of people asking no questions, or small questions."

Ask these *big questions:*

Why is this happening?
How have I contributed to the problem?
Is our religion vital and alive?

Love is not enough. There must be an understanding.

In the training film *The Angry Boy,* the youngster who was filled with bitterness and resentment finally found a friend in the counselor who listened to his interpretation of what life was like. In trying to talk with his mother about his new relationship with the counselor, the boy said, "Dr. Clark loves me."

"Oh," the mother quickly responded, "I love you also, very much!"

"But," said the boy as he rolled his eyes toward the floor, "he understands me!"

6. Take the dial that controls the mental climate and make sure it is set to *positive*.

There are two dial settings: *negative* and *positive*. You can tell if the thermostat is set to cooling—cool air comes out! You'll be chilly. If it's set to heating—you'll feel warm air come out.

If your family mental climate is tuned to the negative there will be complaining, instead of complimenting; there will be griping, instead of gratitude.

Dr. Leslie Parrott writes in *Easy to Live With:*

Some years ago a professor at the University of Pennsylvania conducted a study of dinner table conversations—hiding microphones in 200 different homes to record dinner table conversation. After these were all organized he placed the conversations into *five categories*. In some homes, he said, there was primarily a *monosyllabic terseness* used for getting what one wants. The family went to the table as though it were a refueling stop. Like many car owners, the family members were intent only on getting their own fuel while they ignored as much as possible the attendants and the other people who were also trying to refuel at the same station. The types of monosyllables used most in these conversations were: *more, yes, salt, pepper, please, thanks.* And they were gone! These people did not get angry with one another; they just ignored each other. They acted like no one else existed except themselves.

A *second type* of conversation in some homes centered on *the evil found in family members*. If there were any disciplinary problems to be handled, they were handled at the dinner table in full view of everyone. The food was criticized and bad manners were paraded before everyone. The kind of conversation which went on around this type of table was used primarily to puncture each other's ego, and to drive in barbs which would hurt long after the meal was forgotten. The pressures around this table built up, oftentimes centering on one individual who finally could take it no longer and left the table, often in tears, through a slammed door.

Then there are those, he said, who tend to center their conversation on *the evils of other people outside the family*. Old bones which the family had gnawed before were often refurbished with juicy new tidbits. Family members found fault with the neighbor's children, with everyone they worked with, and the church they attended. In these kinds of families the father and mother were unwilling to accept the fact that there were any problems or shortcomings within themselves. Their policy was that, rather than admit their own faults, they looked for these failures in everybody else. If you don't like Bach or Beethoven, it must be their fault. Lash out at them or anyone else who makes you feel inadequate. This will help build up your feelings of self-righteousness. Soon you delude yourself into feeling you are better than everybody else. Criticizing other people for your own faults tends to make you forget your painful shortcomings.

Only a few families were among the *fourth group,* who kept their conversation on *the positive side of people and things.* And even a smaller portion were in *group five,* who made the dinner table a forum for discussing *political and social issues* instead of personalities and incidentals.

7. Check your Power Center.

Every institution has its Power Center. The Power Center of our society is the family. As the families go —so goes the nation. The Power Center of the retail shopping center is the large department store: if it goes bankrupt, the entire shopping center will fold up. In every church you will find a Power Center. It may be the church board, or it may be the professional staff, or it may be an unorganized group of aggressive, progressive persons who think alike and move things ahead. Where there is no strong and sure Power Center, disintegration will follow.

Consider the universities that have been thrown into turmoil by a power-center confusion.

Students want to run the school.
Faculties want to run the school.

Trustees want to run the school.
Alumni want to run the school.
Administrators want to run the school.

POWER CENTER

Consider the confusion in the power center of many families.

Streets want to run the family.
Schools want to run the family.
Society wants to run the family.
Children want to run the family.
Parents want to run the family.

Who should run the family? Without hesitation the answer must be: Jesus Christ working through the hearts and minds of the parents.

Now then, parents, take this action *now!*

Determine to turn your life over to Jesus Christ. Put God at the Power Center of your life. Live your faith joyously and enthusiastically. Now take control of the family and make it the greatest institution in the world.

2

THE MARRIAGE

Ten Principles for Making Marriage Fun

Your biggest problem here is to believe—*really* believe—that it is possible.

This is especially true if you are tied up in an uptight marriage, or divorced after a horrible hitch with a miserable mate. Before you read on, begin at the starting point. Exercise possibility thinking! Dethrone cynical thoughts from their tyrannical mastery over your morbid marriage moods. Think cynical, bitter, negative, impossibility thoughts and you will reap a sour harvest of icy rejection as you move into your lonely future.

If you plant thistles, you can't expect to harvest grapes. If you plant impossibility thoughts you can't expect to harvest great possibilities.

Launch, then, into Operation Big Switch. That's the exercise of switching your thinking from the negative to the positive. You have the power to change your mental attitude. Do it *now*. Here's how: Let God speak to you assuring you that He has a *new* life, a *new* future, a *new* chance for happiness for you!

"Therefore if any man be in Christ he is a new creature: old things are passed away; behold, all things are become new" (2 Corinthians 5:17).

I am positive that the advice I give in this chapter is going to work for you, if you work at it, for I've lived these principles with my wife for over a fifth of a century. Practice these principles and put fun in your marriage.

1. MIND YOUR MANNERS

The first rule of getting along with anyone is courtesy. It's amazing how we have a natural tendency to be polite when we are in the public eye, while we have an enormous inclination to forget our manners as soon as we close the door of our home behind us and move within a family circle.

Common sense should dictate that we would use our manners most sensitively with the people whose friendship and goodwill are most important to us. You would think, therefore, that if we used our heads, we would be at our best in our own homes and we would be at our worst with those with whom we have no call for continued contact, but such, unfortunately, is rarely the case.

Minding your manners refers to such simple things as cleanliness of body, speech, and dress. It means courtesy, respect and thoughtfulness. It is a husband continuing to open the door of a car for his wife after they have been married many years. It is a man walking side by side with his wife when they are out shopping, instead of walking three or four paces ahead of her. It is a husband thoughtfully offering to take care of many of the little chores that his wife should not be doing alone.

Of first importance, *find out the sensitive area in your mate's life*. There is something that will offend him that you would never suspect would be offensive. Everybody has his pet peeves. For myself, it was when my wife neglected to put the cap on the toothpaste tube the first couple of weeks after we were married.

Husbands, find out what about your life bothers your wife the most. Wives, find out what about your life bothers your husband the most.

Chances are you do not realize what about you is most offensive to your mate. I recently played the marriage game with my wife. I asked her what habit or behavior pattern about my life was most disagreeable to her. I was positive that I knew what her answer would be. I had about three negative factors in my life that I expected her to mention. Instead, she named something that I never thought bothered her at all! We turned the game around and played it the other way, and she had never suspected what qualities in her life I found most potentially disagreeable.

This is probably due to the fact that we just really never know ourselves as others know us. Play the game. Find out what in your life is most disagreeable to your mate. Then, by all means, use your head and know that common decency and good manners would dictate that you correct or neutralize this negative quality, promptly and permanently.

It may be some simple little habit. But remember
that it's the little things we do and the minor words
we say that make or break the beauty of the average
passing day.

2. NEVER STOP COURTING

And what is courting but communicating in depth?
If there is one major cause of marriage breakdown, it
is the breakdown in communications.

"I told you so," he said.

"You did not," she retorted.

"I did, too, tell you," he argued.

"I swear you never said a thing to me about it," she
stoutly contended.

This problem of communications is more acute in
our day and age than ever before. I have to confess
that probably a dozen times a year my wife and I have
a conversation not unlike the conversation in the pre-
ceding paragraph. The problem is that we live in a
time of telephones, radios, doorbells, special delivery
letters, telegrams, daily mail, newspapers, and television. In short, there are thousands of thoughts that are
bombarding our minds in the course of a day's time,
and it is no wonder that we forget to communicate
something to our own mate.

So we now save one night a week to be out alone
together. We reserve this night to go out and eat in
some quiet place where we can have a "staff confer-
ence." We check the calendar for the rest of the week.
She checks my schedule and I check her schedule and

we check together the schedules of our children. At the same time, in a charming, romantic, nondefensive setting, we spend a few hours in an atmosphere where we can open our hearts naturally and honestly to each other and unfold our deeper feelings. As a result we are in tune with each other emotionally and spiritually for another seven days. But we need to have this meeting almost every seven days, even as we need to worship every seven days. Moreover, it keeps us living on a close, friendship level.

> Someone asked me
> To name the time
> Our friendship stopped
> And love began.
>
> Oh, my darling,
> That's the secret.
> Our friendship
> Never stopped.
> —LOIS WYSE

3. MANAGE MONEY OR MONEY WILL MANAGE YOU

Know how to handle money and you will eliminate a major cause of marriage problems. Too many marriages break down because the end and the purpose of life is the almighty dollar. If money becomes an end in itself, you can be sure there is a distortion of values that is bound to create some real problems.

It is still true that *the best things in life are free*.

Those experiences that give you the deepest fulfillment, and deepest love, do not cost a dime.

Since we need money to exist and since money can be a great advantage toward improving our lives, it is important that we know how to handle money.

It is very important that husbands and wives should never commit their total earnings to monthly payments unless they have some kind of a reserve for emergencies. If both the husband and wife are working, do not make the mistake of committing your total earned income to monthly payments. At least, make no long term monthly-payment commitments which depend upon the wife's income, unless these monthly payments are nine months or less!

Manage money or money will manage you. A simple technique is easy to remember—when you have earned your money, put 10 percent aside in a savings program of some type. Give another 10 percent away to Christ and to your church. This does something wonderful to both of you. By saving you are developing a quality of self-discipline through a character-building experience. By giving 10 percent regularly to the church, you will be reducing the intensity of selfishness which is always the root of every argument and human problem. Set 10 percent aside for savings, give 10 percent back to God and to His good work in this world, and live on the 80 percent that remains. If you can't live on the 80 percent that remains, you are living beyond your means!

4. FEEL FREE TO LET YOURSELF GO

Now that you are married in the sight of God and in the sight of society, release yourself utterly and completely in the intimate areas of your marriage. Let yourself fly. Let no shame, no guilt, no inner feelings of embarrassment restrain you from the total and complete enjoyment of marriage.

Now is your opportunity to become a complete person, for when God created the human being, He designed the organism in such a way that we are not complete as a person until we are lost in someone else.

The real joy and delight and pleasure of sex is the sense of being a completely total person. A plant is not complete until it is rooted and growing in soil. When a plant is uprooted from the soil, it is not a complete plant, for it cannot and will not grow.

There is absolutely nothing sinful about enjoying sex. You are married now—enjoy yourself. Let yourself go. You are free to enjoy yourself.

Know that the way to enjoy yourself is never to seek self-satisfaction, but always to seek the satisfaction of someone else. Happiness always comes as a by-product. If you ever set out with the intention of finding pleasure for yourself, you will run into all kinds of frustrations. Live to bring fulfillment, joy and pleasure to your mate, and you will experience the wonderful happy feeling that comes when you see that you have brought true joy to some wonderful person whom you love.

5. GET SET FOR THE ADVENTURE OF DISCOVERING NEW FRIENDS

More than one bride cannot tolerate (as a friend) her husband's best man at the marriage. More than one groom will confess that he just cannot stand (as a close friend) his wife's maid of honor.

Now, if a husband senses that one of his old friends is disagreeable to his wife (and vice versa) there is simply no question about what he must do—he simply cuts off this old friendship. "So long, old buddy, it has been nice knowing you," is the attitude that a husband will take toward a male companion whom he used to know in high school and college, but who now doesn't fit into his married life. Together, husband and wife must build new friendships.

It's very exciting discovering new friends. Most churches have young-married and couples clubs. Here in these social units you can find new friends who will be mutually appreciated by both of you.

Choose the new kind of friends you would like to invite into your home—ones who will unquestionably strengthen your marriage and your love.

We all know that if a teen-ager gets into the right crowd, he or she can turn out to be a wonderful person. But if he or she gets into the wrong crowd, he or she can really get into trouble. Now this social principle never changes with the years! A young married couple can join the right crowd and things can go great—or they can get into the wrong crowd and mess things up in a hurry.

6. ESTABLISH BY-LAWS ON IN-LAWS

Every corporation must establish by-laws. This is one of the first things a new institution must do. When you are united in marriage, you are a corporation, so establish by-laws on in-laws.

Some of the things that these by-laws might contain are: (1) No in-law takes priority in my life over my mate. We will never allow any in-law to come between us. Our love and loyalty to each other is first and foremost. When father and mother give away the bride, something very significant happens. It means that the father and mother admit that they no longer have first place in their daughter's life. It means the husband now has first place in their daughter's life. A change of command and a change of priority of influence takes place. In-laws can come second and third, but never first.

A second by-law for in-laws might be: (2) Never listen to any negative, destructive comment about your mate from your family or your relatives. If your relatives make any negative, critical or nonconstructive comment about your mate, block these thoughts out immediately. Refuse to listen. Change the subject. Leave the room, or these ideas will become poisonous darts infecting your mind with a negativism that will become a perilous poison in your marriage. Husband or wife, if your mother makes some negative remarks in a sly or subtle way about your mate, *don't listen to her!*

7. REMEMBER THAT HAPPINESS DOESN'T COME IN BOTTLES, BOXES OR BAGS

Perhaps no problem is more common in marriage than that of problem-drinking. Today boxes and bags of narcotics are also coming into the picture. Drinking, in one form or another, appears as a contributing factor in almost every problem marriage today. Lots of terrible problems are packaged in very beautiful flasks.

Now if you are about to get married and you have never started social drinking, just remember you don't have to drink to be sociable. You don't have to become a social drinker in order to be successful, happy, and popular in today's world. There are many religions that oppose social drinking. Many religious groups oppose social drinking. It is not uncommon to see a very successful prominent person refuse to drink in a very polite way.

It is a fact that no alcoholic ever took his first cocktail with the intention of becoming an uncontrollable drinker. Because of the increase of alcoholic problems, the concept of voluntary abstinence from alcohol is catching on and spreading across the country today. People are discovering that the safest and the cheapest cure is prevention. The simplest precaution against the drinking problem is voluntary abstinence. It is so simple.

Again and again the story is unfolded in our marriage counseling. Three couples or two couples were having a wonderful evening together, and they got along fine for many weeks, months, or years. Then there was a little social drinking. A husband and another wife had one drink too many, and became flirtatious with each other. When the party broke up, there were feelings of jealousy, resentment and hostility between mates. So the beginning of deterioration established itself like an incurable rot in the marriage, and it all started with what seemed like such innocent social drinking.

Join the smart set! Be a happy, popular, fun-spreading, laughing, nondrinker. Then you can be sure you will never make a drunken fool out of yourself. Remember, happiness doesn't come in bottles.

8. KEEP ON GROWING CLOSER AS THE YEARS GO BY

Be intimate always. Keep no secrets from each other. Honestly share your fears, hopes and dreams. Never let the sun set on a bad feeling. Talk it out and away before you go to sleep. You must open up, or eventually you will blow up.

Make sure you are both genuinely human. There are three kinds of persons. *I to I* persons are ego-centered, selfish personalities who relate only to self-satisfying ideas, offers, and opinions. There is no room for the truly selfish person in a lasting marriage. *I to It* persons are those who derive their main fulfillment from things. Buying, shopping, arranging, admiring, and adoring *things* is what gives their life meaning, purpose, pleasure, and security. *I to You* persons are those who derive emotional fulfillment in relating to people. Pleasure, purpose, and meaning in life are expressed in the enthusiastic sharing of experiences with people. That's being truly human! When Christ lives within a person, the person becomes sensitive to people.

If you will be an *I to You* person you will be able to grow closer to your mate as the years go by.

Make a commitment to continuity. Too many couples enter marriage with a commitment to the temporary, or a commitment to experimentation, or a commitment to a trial period. No wonder, then, that with such an attitude they allow negative feelings to escalate into hard, cold divorce-producing problems.

Put priorities on your values. In marriage, two separate persons bring into a union two separate sets of values. Each should list them on paper, then rate them in order of importance, until there is agreement. I recommend the following scale.

(1) RELIGION should come first. Where it does, you see marriages lasting far longer than where religion is left out. If yours is a mixed marriage, in religion, work to concentrate on the ingredients of your faiths that both can accept. Find God and give Him first place.

(2) THE MARRIAGE CONTRACT must come next. You achieve what you determine under God you *will* achieve. Of course, both mates must agree on this.

(3) CHILDREN come third. If a wife puts her children ahead of her husband, she is courting real trouble for her marriage. Remember, the greatest

and first thing to do for your children is to give them a strong father-mother team! Put the children first and when they're out of the house your husband will go, too.

Now, take action. List your values and assign the priorities.

Give, give in, forgive, and never keep score! And you'll stay close as the years go by. Remember, marriage is not a 50–50 proposition: MARRIAGE IS A 60–40 DEAL.

The husband must take this attitude. "I have to give in 60 percent of the time—she has to give in only 40 percent of the time."

Now the wife must take this attitude. "I have to give in 60 percent of the time—my husband only has to give in 40 percent of the time."

When this attitude prevails, you avoid confrontation—rather, you experience overlapping! Remember, give, give in, forgive and *don't keep score!*

9. KEEP FAITH AND LIVE HAPPILY

The opposite is also true—break faith and you destroy everything. I have in my office an almost worthless old jug that I bought in Hebron. I was carrying it in my flight bag, along with a few rocks that I picked up in the Holy Land. The strap broke, the bag fell and the jug was cracked by the rocks. I was going to throw it away, but decided to glue the cracked vase together again. So I glued it together and I still have it, but there are the scars and the cracks that remind me of its damage. Someone said, "It is easier to get a man on the moon than it is to try to put a broken egg back together again."

Husbands—wives—never break faith with your mate. Break faith and it may be possible to repair the damage, but the scars and cracks will show. Break faith and suspicion comes into the mind. "Suspicion is the most unreliable form of mental activity," Dr. Norman Vincent Peale once wrote. And I would add, it is also the form of mental activity that is almost impossible to uproot once it has established its terrible tentacles in one's thinking.

Again and again, we hear a story that goes something like this: It started as a simple flirtation—a cocktail, a friend at the office—until finally a feeling developed, and then an affair. So infidelity crept into the marriage. The worst thing that can possibly happen in a marriage is the shattering of blind faith.

Shatter faith and you destroy everything. There can be no communication. *You cannot apologize to a person who doesn't believe in you.* They will doubt your sincerity. *You cannot even weep and cry to someone who will not believe in you.* They will think that you are clever enough to squeeze out a tear at the right moment. Break faith and you lose everything. Keep faith and you can talk, compromise, cooperate, give and take, and overcome almost any problem.

10. KEEP LOVE AND YOU HAVE EVERYTHING GOING FOR YOU ALL THE TIME

Remember that there are three levels of love. (1) I want you, therefore I love you. This is the lowest level of love. It is basically selfish. It is hardly more than an animal attraction. (2) I need you, therefore I love you. This is still a very shallow level of love. It is often nothing more than lust. It can be noble and worthy, but it is still self-seeking. (3) You need me, therefore I love you. This is love rising to an unselfish level. This is the kind of love that sets you into a frame of mind where your major purpose in marriage is to bring happiness to your mate. Such a basically unselfish purpose is bound to bring greater joy.

This is the kind of love that will carry you through almost every storm of life.

The only way that I know for this kind of love to come in and stay in a person's heart, is for the Spirit of Christ to come into your life.

You see, we are all human beings, and we are born very selfish and self-centered and egotistic. The Bible calls this sin, which means that we are born with a self-centered will. "I want what I want when I want it, the way I want it. People who get in my way, I do not like. People who frustrate or oppose and stand in my way or build obstacles—these are the people I don't like. Agree with me and I will love you. Disagree with me and I will not love you." This is human nature. This is the way all of us by nature think and feel and act.

Somehow, this self-centered backbone in our spirit

has to be broken. This is why Christians speak of conversion—or being born again. Christ is alive. He can come into a human being and change this attitude basically and fundamentally.

I invite you then to ask Jesus Christ to come and live in your heart and in your life. Simply pray a prayer like this:

Christ, here is my body. I invite You to live in it. Christ, here is my brain. I invite You to think through it. Here is my face. I invite You to glow from it. Christ, here are my eyes. I invite You to look at people through them. Christ, here is my emotional system. I invite You to love people and care for people, using my emotional system.

Christ will begin loving people through you. *Christ loves people,* not first of all because He wants them, or needs them, but because *they need Him.* Again and again, I talk to young people who are about to be married, and they tell me that they are all set. They have lined up an apartment, they have even purchased their furniture. They have a car purchased. They even have an insurance program established, and they have opened a savings account. Some have even joined a church. It would seem as if they are all set for marriage, completely prepared to venture out in life's greatest institutional pursuit.

But again and again, questioning reveals the most important thing is still neglected in their life. Again and again, I find that they have neglected to invite

Jesus Christ to live in their individual lives. Without Christ in your life, you absolutely are not prepared to face life in marriage.

Recently we returned from a vacation in the Middle West. While there, our family was without a car since we travelled by plane. In Iowa, a friend of mine said to me, "I have a car you can use. When you are ready to fly back to California, I will drop around and drive your family to the airport. You can fly home, and I will take my car back to my home."

The day before we left, I took my friend's car and made sure it was all packed. The day of our departure arrived. My friend dropped around. We said our good-byes. We all piled in the car. All seven of us! Mrs. Schuller held Gretchen on her lap. Next to her in the back seat was Jeanne Anne, next to Jeanne Anne was Sheila. In the front seat was my friend, the driver, next to him was my son Robert, and I sat by him holding our two-and-one-half-year-old Carol on my lap. Before we left, my wife and I checked things mentally.

"Do you have all ten suitcases?" my wife asked.

"Yes," I said, "all ten."

"Do you have the plane tickets?" she asked.

"Yep."

"Do you have your billfold and the checkbook?" Again I said, "Yes."

"Do you have the key to our home in California? It would be terrible to get home and find out we didn't have the key to get into our own house." And so we checked everything.

Since we had forgotten nothing, we were all set.

We had a brief word of prayer, and we turned to the driver and said, "Let's go."

He suddenly turned to me and said, "Where is the key to my car?" I was stunned. I had been driving the car for a few days and now had neglected to give the key back to him. Frankly I didn't know where it was. I felt in my pocket. It was not there. "I'll bet it's in your gray pants," my wife said.

"Where are the gray pants?" I asked.

"In the gray suitcase," she said.

I got out of the car, opened the trunk, took out the green suitcase, took out the second green suitcase, took out the briefcase, took out the train case, took out the brown suitcase, took out the blue suitcase, took out Bobby's suitcase, got the gray suitcase out, opened it, and called out to my wife, "Which side is it on?"

"I don't know," she answered. I looked through one side—shirts, socks, extra pair of shoes, etc. No gray pants. I opened the other side of the suitcase, piled through an assortment of neatly folded clothing and finally pulled out my gray trousers. I went through the pockets. No key! So I closed the suitcase and put it back in the trunk along with all the others that I had taken out. I finally got the trunk packed again, pressed the lid down and climbed back in the car. I looked at the family of seven and my driver sitting in a beautiful automobile, unable to go any place simply because we didn't have the car key. What good were the plane tickets without the car key to get there? My friend simply went to the house and made a telephone call to his wife, who arrived about ten minutes later with an extra key she had on her key chain.

The point is, at that moment the most important thing was the car key. Without it, we couldn't get very far.

I say to a husband and to a wife—to a would-be husband and a would-be wife—you may have your plans for a house, a car, a life insurance policy and a savings account, but unless you have made a personal commitment and decision about Jesus Christ, you really do not have the most important thing that you need.

I invite you now to take Christ into *your* life. His Spirit in your life is the key that will spell success in marriage. Let Him be the head of your home, the unseen guest at every meal, the silent listener to every conversation. Remember that He promised, "Every one then who hears these words of mine and does them will be like a wise man who built his house upon the rock; and the rain fell, and the floods came, and the winds blew and beat upon that house, but it did not fall, because it had been founded on the rock" (Matthew 7:24,25).

3

THE WIFE

A Wonderful Wife Makes All the Difference in the World

When the subtitle of this chapter was read by two single adults each commented, "Sounds great—but it's not for me."

Are you a single male adult? This chapter is for you, for you may have a wife some day. Be a possibility thinker!

Are you a single female adult? You, too, may be a wife some day. An older woman, single all her life, was approached by her pastor: "I hear you're getting married!"

She replied with a twinkle, " 'Tain't a word of truth in it, but thank God for the rumor."

Yes, this chapter is for you! It's about wives, and almost every person is one, is married to one, will be one, will be married to one, or is the son or daughter of one.

Of all the persons in the world, no one is more important than that crowd we call *wives*. "Behind every successful man is a great woman," is a famous and truthful statement. Someone else put it this way: "Whether a man winds up with a nest egg or a goose egg may depend on the chick he married."

Bill Vaughn of the Kansas City *Star* made this evaluation:

> People who think up statistics about how much a wife is worth will list baby-sitting at $.50 an hour, secretarial duties at $1.25, laundry at $10 a week, etc. It usually adds up to about $150 a week.
>
> This strikes me as selling the darling considerably short. A good wife is a lawyer. She goes to the automobile salesman and says, "Charlie, you unloaded a terrible car on us which makes funny noises when it starts, which it seldom does, and I am either going to sue or scream quite a bit and maybe throw myself down on the floor of your luxurious showroom and kick my heels." Charlie says, "Lady, we'll fix the car."
>
> This is much better than a husband could do. He'd go in and say, "Uh, Charlie, you don't suppose there's the slightest possibility there's something wrong with this zingy, think-young model you sold me?" Charlie says, "No." The husband says, "I thought not." From then on, the family is stuck with the lemon.
>
> So, on deals like this, I figure the wife is worth a $25,000 retainer as a lawyer. In this capacity she also gets mangled shirts refurbished by the laundry and the insurance company is straight-

ened out on why it should put a new roof on the house.

Wives are also doctors. A husband will come home feeling no particular symptoms except that he is a little weary, and he will get a quick prescription: "What you need is a few fast hands of canasta with Sam and Neva. It will be a grand tonic for the system. We can have dinner on the way over to their house at a medium-priced eatery." And he survives. What do doctors make a year? Put it down for 15 big bills.

In addition, the wife is a psychiatrist. A man says, "I want to go bowling tomorrow night." His wife says, "You're nuts." If there is only one of these sessions a week, at $50 each, it's still $2500 a year.

Then take marriage counselors. Wives are the greatest marriage counselors in the world. A husband will say, "There's something wrong with our marriage." She answers, "It's your fault." What's left to be said? Make it another $25,000 a year.

Wives are also other highly paid professionals —tax advisers and engineers, for example. The way I figure it, the average wife is worth easy $185,000 a year.

(Condensed from "The Worth of a Wife.")

Now for the million dollar question: What does a man really want in a woman?

A CONSECRATED CONCUBINE

A man wants someone who can fulfill his biological needs. So he seeks a sexual partner. Every healthy husband needs a concubine, not in the usual immoral sense of a sexual mate outside of marriage or in addition to a legal wife. The truth is every wife should provide her husband with the sexual pleasures normally solicited from a concubine. "My wife is my one and only concubine," one satisfied man said to me recently.

We must never forget that God is responsible for this thing called *sex*. God designed and created male and female. "And God saw everything that he had made and beheld it was very good" (Genesis 1:31). Commenting on this verse, Charlie Shedd once added, "And among the best of God's good things is sex at its best."

Many counselors agree that sex is a primary cause of problems in marriage. The challenge to wives is to become successful playmates with their husbands. Dr. Marion Hilliard wrote about a patient, a minister's wife, who had come to her sheepishly with her problem. She and her husband enjoyed one another once a week, on Sunday nights. It left her exhausted the next morning when she had to face an enormous weekly washing.

"I've tried to persuade him that this is very difficult for me," the minister's wife complained, "but it's no use. Is there something I could do about it?"

"Certainly," replied Dr. Hilliard promptly, "wash on Tuesdays."

The wife is her man's one and only concubine—consecrated by marriage!

A CONFIDANT

Deep though the biological needs may be, even deeper are man's social needs. He needs one person to whom he can truly open up his heart, his hurt, his hopes. Man wants in a woman someone who can listen to him as he thinks his way through his dreams, and aches his way through his problems.

Marriage, with a commitment to confidential continuity, provides man with a mate to whom he can totally expose himself—body and soul! If he feels assured that this wife is his and his alone for life, then he can trust her with his private, intimate feelings. You do not totally trust a person with whom the relationship has a strong possibility of impermanence.

A COMPANION

What does a man want in a woman? He wants a warm friend, an understanding companion.

A study was made of fifteen hundred marriages and the number one complaint of men regarding wives was that they talk too much and don't listen enough.

One man said, "My wife can talk herself out of anything but a phone booth."

One wife complained to her husband about the bad manners of her new neighbor. "If that woman yawned once, Albert, while I was talking, she yawned a dozen times." To which Albert replied, "Maybe she wasn't yawning, dear, maybe she was trying to say something."

In most adulterous triangles this is the pattern. Wandering husband (or wandering wife): "I first became attracted to the third party because he (she) was so understanding. It wasn't a physical, sexual thing. It was simply that he (or she) wanted to listen to me and it seemed my wife (husband) never really wanted to listen. It started out as a warm companionship— that's all. Somewhere it got out of hand."

In the May, 1971, *Good Housekeeping,* Virginia Graham offered five suggestions on how to stay happily married. I particularly like her final point.

Virginia Graham's Five Easy Steps to Magnificent Matrimony

First, be sure you take a long, hard look at your fiancé's family before you say yes. Basically, *he* will be what *they* are *now*.

Second, make certain either that you genuinely *do* like what he likes, or that whatever it is won't be hard to live with for the rest of your life.

Third, don't be dogmatic or inflexible. . . .

Fourth, put your troubles and tears away for tomorrow.

And fifth, try to look ahead to a day in the distant future when someone will ask you how you've managed to stay happily married for so long. I hope you'll be able to answer the way I do: "It's easy," I say. "I married my best friend."

In "Woman's Guide to Better Living 52 Weeks a Year," Dr. John A. Schindler, the counselor, writes wisely: "Love is the combination of sex and deep friendship. The trouble with a lot of love is that it is mostly sex and very little friendship."

A CONSCIENCE

Most men might not admit it, but they do expect the women to be the consciences of their lives and their communities.

Businessman: "My wife doesn't care how good-looking my secretary is as long as he's efficient."

My wife is my conscience. How I respect her for it! How she helps me! But being the conscience doesn't mean that a wife is to *change* or *convert* her husband.

Ruth Graham, wife of Billy Graham, said: "A wife's job is to love her husband, not convert him."

But retain the spirit that can advise, or gently correct. When the wife ceases to be the symbol of The Ideal, all of society will begin to deteriorate. Be a kind conscience!

John Boyle O'Reilly asks in a poem, "What Is the Good?"

> "What is real good?"
> I asked in musing mood.
>
> Order, said the law court;
> Knowledge, said the school;
> Truth, said the wise man;

Pleasure, said the fool;
Love, said a maiden;
Beauty, said the page;
Freedom, said the dreamer;
Home, said the sage;
Fame, said the soldier;
Equity, the seer;
Spoke my heart full sadly;
"The answer is not here."
Then within my bosom
Softly this I heard:

"Each heart holds the secret;
Kindness is the word."

A Creative Climate Controller

What a man wants in a wife is someone who can set the mental climate control to positive thinking. Be a possibility thinking woman.

A highway patrolman stopped a speeding woman who had one of the most positive excuses he ever heard. "This highway is so dangerous I was hurrying to get off of it."

The wife can be her husband's biggest booster. Wives: Nothing is more important than building his male ego. Nothing is more disastrous than neglecting to boost, bolster and build his ego!

For this reason the most important quality of a successful wife is Possibility Thinking. If a man is dreaming, only to have his wife squelch his dreams and throw cold water on his exciting plans, the marriage is headed for the rocks. No man will ever leave, or stop loving, a positive thinking wife who feeds his enthusiasm and self-confidence.

How can you be a confidence-generating woman? Listen again to Virginia Graham as she wrote in *Good Housekeeping*.

Everyone needs what I call a Chinese Room to which you can retreat and more or less get reacquainted with yourself. Go in there alone and make a mental market list of what you're doing right, and what you're doing wrong.

In your Chinese Room, you may come to realize that while you keep your house in perfect running order, and you never forget to put eggs, butter and bacon on your market list, and you never let the flowers wilt in a vase, you may be a lot less careful about how you're running your marriage. A big mirror in your Chinese Room is a must. Take a good look in it. You may see that not only your hair needs a touch-up, but your mind does, too. You may feel that you're over-hubbied, but maybe you're really over-hobbied, and hubby hasn't been over-happy for quite a while. Come out of your Chinese Room with the words "I love you" at the top of your mental market list. Then say the words out loud.

If your mate seems hard of hearing, it's only probably that he hasn't heard the phrase in so long, he can't immediately recognize it for what it is.

[Virginia's example of someone who has a Chinese Room is Lucille Ball.] When Lucy married Gary Morton, he was a stand-up comedian. She, of course, was a giant, a monumental star, and she still is. But for five years, Gary patiently went about the task of learning Lucy's business. She, in her turn, visited her Chinese Room, and learned how to relinquish her hold on the business end of her vast talent. Now, when you have dinner with Lucy and Gary, frequently she never opens her mouth, unless it's to agree with Gary.

And he says of Lucy, "She may be my boss during the day, but at night, she's my wife."

You create a positive mental climate by being a cheerful happy woman. Pity the man who, tired from a day's work, has to come home to a depressed, fatigued, self-pitying woman. Be proud of your role as a wife and a homemaker. What could be more important!

Catherine Menninger, wife of the famous Dr. William Menninger relates in a *Reader's Digest* article:

I remember one night when I lay in bed fretting for hours over my humdrum existence, and envying the exciting, worthwhile lives of the (to me) glamorous nurses who worked with Dr. Will.

Sensing that I was awake, my husband asked what was wrong. I burst into tears and began pouring out my frustrations. He listened quietly and then asked, "Cay, do you really believe that raising our three boys, helping them develop into men with healthy minds and bodies, isn't important work? Nurses can try to cure illness, but you have a chance to prevent it."

You create a positive mental climate by being patient. (That's putting off till tomorrow what you'd mess up by doing it today.) Practice the art of tactfulness. (That's changing the subject without changing your mind.) Above all, cultivate the habit of acceptance. (That's loving persons as the imperfect human beings they really are. It's the exercise of *mature love*.)

Dr. Haim Ginott wrote in *Between Parent and Teenager:*

Love is not just feeling and passion. Love is a system of attitudes and a series of acts which engender growth and enhance life for both lover and beloved. Romantic love is often blind. It acknowledges the strength but does not see the weakness in the beloved. In contrast, mature love accepts the strength without rejecting the weakness. In mature love neither boy nor girl tries to exploit or possess the other. Each belongs to himself. Such love gives the freedom to unfold and to become one's best self. Such love is also a com-

mitment to stay in the relationship and attempt
to work out difficulties even in times of anger
and agony. Love and sex are not the same emotion, but the wise learn to combine them.

Now generate a positive mental climate by encour-
aging your husband to succeed. Know your husband,
support your husband. Be his biggest booster. Be
proud of him and let that pride show! Be a possibility
thinker. Be careful in your response to his positive
ideas.
Don't say:

It can't be done.
We can't afford it.
I'm too tired.
But the children . . .
We don't have the time.
It's impossible.

Do say:

Sounds great.
How can we swing it?
Let's see how we can possibly do it.
Let's find a way to do it.
Let's think and think until we think up a solution.

To become this kind of person put God in your life.
Real religion makes all the difference in the world.

A rabbi and a soapmaker went for a walk together. The soapmaker said, "What good is religion? Look at the trouble and the misery in the world after thousands of years of religion. If religion is true, why should this be?"

The rabbi said nothing. They continued walking until he noticed a child playing in the gutter. The child was filthy with mud and grime. The rabbi said, "Look at that child. You say that soap makes people clean. We've had soap for generation after generation, yet look how dirty the youngster is. Of what value is soap? With all the soap in the world that child is still filthy. How effective is soap anyway?"

The soapmaker protested and said, "But Rabbi, soap can't do any good unless it's used."

"Exactly," replied the rabbi, "so it is with religion."

Religion isn't effective unless used—and it must be used—day after day, after day, after day! Real religious power will come into your life and make you a genuinely attractive woman if you will let Christ come into your heart and life.

Robert Null, M.D., a prominent Southern California eye specialist and a member of my church, has said to me, "I've looked into the eyes of thousands of women and believe me, I can tell by their eyes if they have Christ in their hearts!"

The woman who is alive in Christ sparkles, twinkles, and is a frisky, peppy person. She never grows old. Happy wrinkles may come around her eyes, but the eyeballs never wrinkle. They sparkle with the look of a teen-ager, into the eighties and nineties!

Now, good reader, as you look at this page, Jesus Christ knocks at the door of your heart. Let Him come into your life *now*. He says: "Behold, I stand at the door and knock; if anyone hears my voice and opens the door, I will come in . . ." (Revelation 3:20).

Do it now. Kneel down and pray!

4

THE HUSBAND

Eight Words of Wisdom for Husbands and Fathers

"I don't know what I'm doing wrong, Dr. Schuller," the distraught husband and father said to me, adding, "but I'm not getting along with my wife or my kids. I've come to the conclusion it must be my fault." After careful analysis I offered him a prescription of Eight Words of Wisdom for Husbands and Fathers. They worked a miracle in his life. Now let them work wonders for you.

1. THINK POSITIVELY

Think positive thoughts and positive things will happen to you.

". . . whatever a man sows that he will also reap." (Galatians 6:7)
"Cast your bread upon the waters, for you will find it after many days." (Ecclesiastes 11:1)
". . . the measure you give will be the measure you get." (Matthew 7:2)

These Bible verses illustrate the law of proportionate return. Life is a rubber ball—whatever you throw out bounces back to you. Positive things happen to positive-thinking people.

I remember a father who came in to see me because his child had really gone off the deep end. He said, "I don't know what we did wrong. We taught him not to smoke and not to drink. We taught him not to swear and we taught him not to steal."

I interrupted and said, "I think that is your problem. You didn't train up the child in the way in which he *should* go. You tried to train up your child in the way in which he *should not* go."

Miracles happen when positive thinking takes over. Charlie Shedd, in one of his marvelous books (*Letters to Karen*) tells about a happily married couple named Bob and Helen. When they were asked the secret of their marriage joy they answered

We had a terrible time when we were first married. In fact, we even talked about calling it quits. Then we read something that gave us an idea. We decided to make a list of all the things we didn't like about each other. Of course, it was hard, but Helen gave me hers and I gave her mine. It was pretty rough reading. Some of the things we had never said out loud or shared in any way.

Next, we did something which might seem foolish, so I hope you won't laugh. We went out to the trash basket in the backyard and burned

those two lists of bad things. We watched them
go up in smoke and put our arms around each
other for the first time in a long while.

Then we went back into the house and made a
<u>list of all the good things we could dig up about</u>
<u>each other.</u> This took some time, since we were
pretty down on our marriage. But we kept at it
and when we finished we did another thing which
might look silly. Come on back to the bedroom
and I'll show you.

It was a neat room, lots of light, and a happy
spread on the big old bed from grandma's house.

But at the focal point on that bedroom wall
were two plain maple frames, and in them what
do you suppose?

In one was the list of the good things Helen
could see in Bob. In the other was his scribbled
list of her virtues. That's all there was. Just two
scratchy lists behind glass.

If we have any secret, I guess this is it. We
agreed to read these things at least once a day.
Of course, we know them by heart now. I
couldn't begin to tell you what they've done for
me. . . . Funny, too, the more I consider the
good she sees in me the more I try to be like that.
And when I really understood her good points
I tried all the harder to build on these. Now I
think she's the most wonderful person in the
world. I guess she sort of likes me, too. . . .

2. Try Positively

The positive thought must be followed, consistently, by positive effort. Positive trying must follow positive thinking. Too many defeated people are like the man who said: "I've got so much to do I don't know where to start, so I'll sit down first and take a rest and then that'll be done, at any rate." The truth is we generally succeed at something when we really have a burning desire to achieve. Where there's a will, there's a way.

Two men were playing golf on Sunday and doing very badly. The first one said, "I guess I should have stayed home and gone to church."

The second addicted golfer replied, "I couldn't have gone to church anyway. My wife is sick in bed."

I know too many fathers today who are trying to get ahead financially, and they are trying to get ahead professionally. But they are not trying with the same passion and fervor to be a success as a husband and father.

Anything worthwhile takes time, effort, and enthusiasm. There are people who are failing in daily life because they think positively but don't try with a passion.

From another excellent book, *Letters to Phillip,* Charlie Shedd tells this story.

> I used to hunt ducks with a man who had a "thing" about his guns. He also had a "thing" about my gun. . . . In fact, my gun even had

some scratches on the brown part. It also had some terrible stuff called "pitting" in the barrel and he said this was because I didn't clean it first thing when I got home after a hunt.

But there were some good reasons why I kept hunting with this firearm perfectionist. He was a member of the best duck lease on the river and I wasn't. He was also chairman of the board at our church and we could talk business to and fro. The third reason wasn't so good. He was having trouble with his wife and I hoped we might be able to save the marriage.

But we couldn't. Finally, she gave up. They got a divorce. It was one of those cases that would make a grown man cry. There he would sit in his beautiful den—antelope heads, stuffed pheasant, lush white rug made from the hide of a mountain goat, cabinet full of beautiful guns all polished with oil that smelled like bananas.

He would stand there by the case taking them out and handling them with tender, loving care. Then he would remember the way my gun looked and take off again on one of his diatribes about the care of guns. This never failed to shame me and I would go home determined to get out my gun and clean it like it had never been cleaned before.

But do you know what happened? When I arrived home, she would be waiting for me at the door. So we would sit down on our rocking love seat, hold hands, visit and like that. In less time than it takes to look into her eyes, I completely forgot my noble resolve to love my gun with more devotion.

The other day as I was thinking back on all this, a great idea occurred to me. Funny, isn't it, how we so often get these brilliant thoughts too late?

What happened was that my banana-oil brother would always include in his lectures at least one reference like this: "I just can't understand how a man could invest so much in a gun and then let it go to pot!"

The thought that came to me was, "Why didn't I figure up how much it cost him to get his wife? Courtship expenses, movies, flowers, dinners, gifts, postage, the wedding. All the food she's eaten through the years, clothes she's bought, medicine. It really would be a tidy sum, wouldn't it?"

Then I could have said, "My dear Whoozit! You are absolutely right! Let us now turn your brilliant observation to other things. Isn't a man a fool to invest so much in marriage and then let it go to pot?"

3. TOUCH TENDERLY

The positive thought leads to the positive try and the positive try leads to the positive touch.

"All I want from my husband is really not much more than my dog wants from him," she said to me in a counseling session one day. She explained, "When my husband comes home my dog is there waiting for three things: first, a look, and when my husband looks at him he wags his tail; and then he wants a word, 'Hi, Collette.' A look, a word, and finally, a touch."

"A look, a word, and a touch," she summarized, "is all I really want from my husband."

Touching is one of our five natural senses and is consequently an enormously powerful vehicle of communication.

A father and husband who complained that "he didn't feel close to his family anymore" had a breakthrough when he followed this advice that I gave him.

"Go to your children's and to your wife's closets and drawers," I ordered, "and touch their clothes. Touch the contents of their drawers. Touch their private things. Feel them. Fondle them. Hold them. Now touch their faces. Feel their inner life warmly vibrating through your fingertips. Also keep in close spiritual touch," I added, "on a daily basis—by contacting them by telephone and simply checking to see how they are."

This leads me to the next words of wisdom.

4. Talk Positively

To build close relationships, keep in close touch by keeping communication lines open. To keep in close touch requires time to talk positively and privately.

Learn to talk creatively and you're well on the way to success in your husband-father role.

A husband is someone who talks to you from the other end of the house with his head in the closet while you are running water in the sink, and then says that you don't listen to him.

Ogden Nash had this wise word of advice to talking husbands.

> To keep your marriage brimming,
> With love in the loving cup,
> Whenever you're wrong, admit it!
> Whenever you're right, shut up.

Dr. Henry Poppen is a wise friend and associate pastor. He spent forty years in overseas work. He was an enormous success in communications. "What's your secret?" I asked one day.

His answer was power-packed. "Three words," he answered. "Be *friendly*. Be *frank*. Be *firm*." I have followed this as a husband and father and it works wonders.

By all means be a positive talker. Be an inspiring person, not a complaining parent. Be an uplifting conversationalist, not a negative grumbler. Let your words inspire, illuminate, uplift, and amuse your household, and the entire mental climate will become electric with happiness and joy. May your children grow old remembering Dad as someone who always cheered them on saying, "You can do it, son! Of course you can. You have the possibilities within you and I'll help see to it that they come out!"

Now create opportunities to talk privately with your wife and each of your children. I deliberately carve out of my busy schedule the occasions to be alone with my children on a personal, private level. It may be in their bedroom, in my bedroom, or in my car. We seek out a mental environment which is conducive to the sharing of intimacies. I make time to pray privately alone with each of my children periodically. It's beautiful! It's absolutely the most rewarding value in my life—these private times! How often? Well, it depends. I'm sensitive to their moods, as well as to the emotional needs within myself. A sensitive man will feel the need within his wife, a child, or himself for a private talk. Respond promptly and forthrightly to these feelings.

When you take time to talk, also take time to practice the next word of wisdom, too.

5. Tune In Positively

Tune in and listen to what members of your family are trying or wanting to say to you. I made this resolution to my wife and children.

I PROMISE TO LISTEN WHEN I HEAR YOU

Perhaps they have legitimate complaints, like the customer of a do-it-yourself catalog firm. The disgruntled client sent this complaining letter.

I built a birdhouse according to your stupid plans. Not only is it too big, but it keeps blowing out of the tree.

—Signed, *Unhappy*

The reply came back.

Dear Unhappy. Sorry, we accidentally sent you a sailboat blueprint. If you think you are unhappy, you should see the guy who came in last in the yacht club regatta in a leaky birdhouse.

By all means be man enough to admit it if you've made a mistake. Apologize. *I'm sorry* are miracle-working words.

I remember the day I had a very harsh argument with my eldest daughter, Sheila, who was a junior in high school at the time. I was rushing to get to the office and she was rushing to get to school. While I was driving her to school, I gave her an extreme verbal lashing. As I dropped her off in front of the high school, said goodbye, and watched her go into the school, I noticed that she was trembling. This really bothered me. I parked my car and prayed. If you pray honestly, you begin by asking, "How can I improve myself?"

I came to the conclusion that I was not behaving like a Christian. So I called up the high school office and contacted the school principal, requesting, "My daughter is enrolled in your school. I must see her this

noon at the lunch hour. Please grant me permission."
Permission was granted.

As Sheila later told some of her high school friends,
"I came down the steps and the principal was there
and said, 'Sheila, your dad is waiting outside to see
you.' "

As she came outdoors I met her with a smile, took
her hand, and said, "Sheila, I certainly am not proud
of the way we handled the situation—particularly the
way I handled it. I want to apologize. I just don't think
I acted like a Christian. There was no excuse for your
behavior—but neither was there an excuse for mine.
Let's go out and have lunch."

I picked out a very fine place with linen napkins
and we had a beautiful lunch. (This was the very first
time that just the two of us went out for lunch together.) Before the lunch was served, we held hands
and we had a prayer. I asked God to forgive me, and
He did. I forgave myself, and my daughter forgave
me. Sheila has told many people that she and I both
felt that this was one of the most rewarding moments
in our lives. We were both very honest in our explo-
sions. We were both very honest in our confessions
of missing the mark. And we were both very honest in
our forgiving!

6. Train Them in Positive Morality

This particular word, of course, applies to the father
role.

In Colorado one day, a great tree fell down. It was

a sapling when Columbus landed at San Salvador. It had been struck by lightning fourteen times and it had survived storms, defied earthquakes, and mountain slides. In the end tiny beetles killed it. They bored under the bark, dug into its heart, ate away its mighty fibers, and down toppled the great king of the forest.

The United States of America is in the gravest danger of falling from the spreading rot of social immorality. Moral character is the skeletal system of a personality, an individual, an institution, a nation.

When the Ten Commandments are violated, openly, you can expect collapse.

What is morality? It is making a decision on what is *right,* not on what is *pleasurable.* The moral person never acts upon "What would I like to do?" rather on "What is the right thing to do?"

Teach your children morality and they will surely be successful persons. By necessity, this involves some powerful positive *nos!* The secretive billionaire Howard Hughes searched for five men who could be his most trusted, intimate aides. He selected five members of the Mormon Church, knowing he could trust them morally.

"Follow God's example in everything you do just as a much loved child imitates his father" (Ephesians 5:1 LB).

"Commit your work to the Lord, then it will succeed" (Proverbs 16:3 LB).

"Train up a child in the way he should go and when he is old he will not depart from it" (Proverbs 22:6 LB).

7. TACKLE PROBLEMS POSITIVELY

Now practice possibility thinking as you face personal and family problems. They're bound to come! Remind yourself—and remind your wife and children —that success is not escaping problems but facing them creatively.

Charley Boswell was a halfback and outfielder at the University of Alabama before World War II. Shortly after Charley graduated in 1940, he was drafted into the army.

In the European theater, he was a rifle company commander. On November 30, 1944, he commandeered a tank, attached a trailer and set out for a nearby German village and American supply depot in search of food and ammo.

A German 88 shell hit the tank, setting it afire. "I got out, but I saw one of the crew was still inside. I went back, pushed him out, and just as I got out of the tank it was hit again. I woke up in the hospital blinded," Boswell said.

Months later, at Valley Forge Hospital, near Philadelphia, he tried bowling. The first time, he fell down and the ball landed two alleys away.

So, he tried horseback riding. As he was riding through the woods, the horse ran under a tree and a branch knocked Boswell to the ground.

The next day, Corporal Kenny Gleason, a former assistant pro from Charlotte, N.C., said to Boswell, "Captain, I'm going to teach you to play golf."

Boswell recalled, "I was really depressed because of my failures at bowling and horseback riding. I really let him have it. How could a blind man play golf when he couldn't even see the ball?" Boswell continued, "But he kept after me and I agreed. He saved me. I learned to play golf."

How well he learned was demonstrated at a local country club.

The first hole at Yorba Linda Country Club stretches out 442 yards. It is so long it strikes terror into the heart of the average golfer who believes he'll be lucky to escape with a bogey 5.

But that first hole sends no tremors through the arms of Charley Boswell, with his handicap of 21. Of course, he can't see the green in the distance, nor can he see the golf ball.

Charley just says, "Point me, I'll put the ball in the hole."

And he does. Boswell, fifty-four, has won the National Blind Golfers' Tournament seventeen times.

Boswell tuned-up for his round by playing a few holes. On the first hole, he took a six, but so did everyone else in the foursome, including Watkins. (His close friend, Waverly Watkins, has a handicap of five).

Even a blind golfer needs a hole or two to warm up, and after slightly pushing his tee shot on the second hole, Charley was in the groove.

He hit good fairway woods on the second hole (402 yards), third (375), and fourth (420). All three shots were in line with the flag, but stopped from five to fifteen yards short of the green.

Charley parred the second hole, but got bogeys on the third and fourth holes. He should have had pars, but for the treachery and fickleness of putts. A five-footer turned uphill and a fourteen-footer smacked the back of the cup and popped out!

It was a good performance for a blind man working with an inexperienced pointer. Watkins hadn't assisted Charley since Boswell's last trip west a year ago.

On every shot, Watkins put the club to the ball, pointing it in the proper direction. Then Boswell gripped the club, set his feet and hit the ball. He never once missed the ball.

On chip shots and putts, Watkins walked Boswell from his ball to the pin so he could get the feel of the distance. On chips, his distance and accuracy are excellent.

On long putts, he is also walked the shot. On putts of four or five feet, he touches the ball with his club, then squats down to feel the hole. When he putts from this distance, he is deadly.

He hits the ball better than a golfer with a handicap of twenty-five, but his scores don't improve, because, like a lot of other guys, he finds business interferes with his golf.

He's a busy man in the business world of Alabama. He has an insurance firm, an outfit that manufactures personalized golf balls, and another that makes golf gloves.

Got problems? It's possible to solve them creatively.

8. Trust Positively

Now move ahead through life with a vital, happy, positive religious faith. Believe in God and be an inspiring father. Find faith. Live that faith. Practice that faith. Let that faith color your whole personality and you'll be a successful husband and father.

Lou Little was football coach at Georgetown University. The college president came to him one day and, naming a student, said, "Lou, do you know this fellow?"

"Sure," Lou answered, "he's been on my squad four years. I've never played him. He's good enough—he's just not motivated."

"Well," the president continued, "we just heard that his father died. Will you break the news to him?"

The coach put his arm around the boy in a back room, "Take a week off, son, I'm sorry." It was Tuesday. Friday, Coach Little came into his locker room to see the student back and suiting up. "What are you doing back already?" Little inquired.

"The funeral was yesterday, coach. So I came back. You see, tomorrow's the big game and I've got to play in it."

"Wait a minute, son," Little said, "you know I've never started you."

"But you will start me tomorrow and you won't be sorry," the moist-eyed boy stated firmly.

Softening, the coach decided that if he won the tossup he would use the boy on the first play. He couldn't do any damage on the first return. Well,

Georgetown won the toss. On the first play this father-less boy came tearing down the field like a tornado. Coach Little, shocked, left him in for another play. He blocked, he tackled, he passed, he ran. He utterly won the ball game that day for Georgetown University.

In the locker room Coach Little, perplexed, asked, "Son, what happened?"

The happy, perspiring victor said, "Coach, you never knew my dad, did you? Well, sir, he was blind and today was the first time he ever saw me play."

Be this kind of a father: Find a faith, and live it. When times seem darkest, your family will rise up and honor you!

5

THE TEEN-AGERS

Ten Tips for Teens

Do you know what you really want more than anything else in the world? Chances are you don't. Many
adults are not aware that what they want more than
life itself is a wonderful feeling of self-love.

He sat in my study with his long curly hair, untidy
clothes, and a sad face with hollow eyes. We made
small talk for awhile, but I could see that his mind
was miles away. We were not making contact at all,
until I asked him bluntly, "Why do you have long
hair?"

Suddenly he came alive and answered immediately,
"Long hair makes me feel tall."

"Do you really *want* long hair?"

"Yes, I want long hair very much."

"Are you sure it's *long hair* that you *really want?*
Or is it the tall feeling that you are really after?"

"I never thought of it that way. I know it's the tall
feeling I like."

"Do your friends in school have long hair?"

"Yes. The kids I hang around with all have long hair."

"What do you think they would think if you had a trim, short haircut in the style of your father?"

"*Yeeck!*"

"What you really want is to be accepted by your friends. When you feel you are really *in* with them, you feel tall. You think the long hair proves that you are *in* with them. It's not long hair that you want, it's being accepted by those with whom you feel safe and secure."

"I never thought of that. You may be right."

"How would you like it if your dad started growing long hair like you have?"

"I don't know. I'm not sure."

"You're not sure, because you really wouldn't like that."

"What do you mean?"

"Do you feel good or bad when you are away from your parents and out with the gang?"

"I feel good when I am out with the other guys."

"So you feel good when you are free from your parents?"

"I guess so."

"So your long hair makes you feel different from your father. It makes you feel separated from your father. It gives you a feeling of freedom from your father. And I don't think you would be very happy if your father wore long curls. You'd probably start cutting your own hair the way he now styles his."

"I never thought of that. You may be right."

"What you are trying to do is to discover yourself. You want to know who you are. You are sixteen years old—what we call an adolescent."

"What does that mean?"

"An adolescent is someone who is not exactly sure what he is. At times, he thinks he is an adult. He thinks this because he has a big body. But emotionally he often feels like a preteen-age youngster—insecure, craving acceptance by others, and wanting to be loved. Most of all, he wants to be able to love himself, and he cannot really love himself until he knows himself. That's why you want to feel free from your father and mother. A person discovers who he is when he is free. But if you are simply doing what all of the others in your gang do, you still are not free. You are copying them. You are following them. You are trying to be what they are. If you are only imitating others, you are not really being yourself. So you are still not free to discover who the *real* you really is."

The session went on for a considerable length of time, and he discovered that what he really wanted was self-respect, self-esteem, self-love.

1. Close the Generation Gap

So my Number One tip for teens who want to learn to love themselves is: *Try to identify with your parents —don't try to escape from them.* If you want to know who you are, and this is necessary before you can really feel secure with yourself, you must also know your parents, for you are a part of your parents, an extension of their life, and more like them than you realize.

You will never be totally free from your parents and you might just as well try to learn to know them. Get acquainted with them, because they will always be with you. You may leave home, you may get married, your parents may even die, but you will never totally escape from them.

A popular psychiatrist, Eric Berne, has written a best-selling book titled *Games People Play*. Here he explains that every person has at least three ego states. There is a child-ego state, which explains why many adults sometimes act like little children—pouting, fighting, screaming.

As the child remains a part of our personalities all our lives, so our parents remain a part of our personalities all our lives. Many times in life you may find yourself acting exactly as your father would have acted. You may suddenly and shockingly say to yourself, "Boy, if that wasn't just like Dad!" This is the parent-ego state in operation. You have not only part of your father's and mother's physical characteristics —you have the eyes, the slope of the shoulders, the walk, the nose of your father or your mother—but you also bring with you through life, more than you will ever know, your father's and mother's spirit.

So, if you have to live with them, mentally, emotionally, and psychologically all your life, it makes sense that you learn to know them, understand them, and get along with them; or you will be fighting them as they exist within yourself all the days of your life.

Try to understand the reasons why they act the way they do.

Build self-love by building bridges of understanding with your father and your mother.

2. GET EDUCATED ABOUT EDUCATION

You will build self-respect, self-esteem, and self-love when you realize that you are not stupid. A teen-ager who drops out of high school, or refuses to give himself a chance to develop his inner potential through a college education, is easily tearing up a $100,000 bill. There is no doubt that a high school and college education is easily worth over $100,000. Money, in and of itself, does not build real self-love, but it can be a very important tool which you can use to build self-esteem. If you use money only to buy big cars and houses to impress people in order to feed your self-worth, then money will be woefully inadequate; but if you look upon money as something you can use to help people who need help, to educate and train your own children so they can be everything they could possibly be, then money becomes very important in building self-love. We love ourselves when we help others to become what they should be.

Money builds hospitals. Money pays for scientific research which will heal the sick. Money is important. You owe it to yourself to earn the most money possible in the best possible way in order to give the most money to the great causes of our time.

I counseled a young man who was tempted to drop

out of college because, he said, "I have a part-time job and they want me to work full-time. They will pay me $600 a month!" To this young man that sounded like a fortune.

"You know," I said to him, "that if you'll spend the next three years completing your college work you will earn far more than $7,200 a year for the next three years? If you will spend the next three years in college you will earn well over $120,000! That's $40,000 a year!"

"What do you mean?" he said.

"It is a proven fact that the average college graduate will earn $3,000 more a year in his forty years of earning power, because he has a college education. That means that if you complete your college work you will, in effect, be paid a total of $120,000 for three years of study. You might say that it's placed in a special bank account for you and will come back to you at the rate of $3,000 a year for the next forty years," I pointed out to him.

"Man!" he said, "I can't afford to drop out." And he didn't.

Self-love is achieved when we discover the talents that God has placed within us. When we are faithful to the highest of our capabilities, we have an immense sense of self-worth. That is the real purpose and end of an education.

To love is to meet someone whom you respect. You will come to know yourself, respect yourself and admire yourself when you discover the potential that is within you.

3. You Owe Your Country a Living

You discover yourself in responsibility. You have inherited citizenship in your country. This means that citizenship carries with it a responsibility as well as a privilege. There is always the danger of accepting the privileges without assuming the responsibilities, but this is a way of living that will never lead to self-discovery or self-appreciation.

It will be wise for you to understand what an inheritance is. An inheritance is not a gift—it is a trust. A trust is something that is given to you to take care of and pass on to others.

I met a young man who was getting ready to drop out of school because, "My dad is pretty rich. He'll be dying one of these days, and I will inherit everything he's got." The boy who was talking was seventeen years old. His father was only forty-one.

"You must realize your father may very likely and possibly live to be ninety years of age," I told him. "Where will you be if he lives to be ninety?"

He had a shocked look on his face when he answered, "Golly, that would make me sixty-seven!"

If you depend upon family inheritance you will never be motivated to unlock your own potential, which is the only way to real self-worth. I couldn't resist a final admonishment to this young man. "If and when you receive the family inheritance, remember that it really doesn't belong to you. It belongs to the family which came before you and will continue after you. It is not your gift. You did not work for it. But it has been placed in your hands as a trust. You may use it if you really need it, but otherwise you are to build upon it and pass it on to your children, so they can pass it on to their children."

Apply this principle of inheritance to your citizenship. You are a citizen of the United States of America; you have inherited the freedom to think and talk and work. Many young people are living in countries where they do not have the freedom which you have inherited. Assume your responsibility to keep your country alive by protecting it from dangers from without and within. Develop a positive and healthy patriotism and you will have a greater sense of personal identity and personal worth.

4. LEARN TO DISTINGUISH BETWEEN LUST AND LOVE

Lust is only the stimulation and exercise of the animal sexual drive. Animal sex looks upon the opposite sexual partner as a *thing*. When sexual energies are released in real love, the sexual partner is not looked upon as an object, but as a person. When a man describes a woman merely with the term *female,* he is thinking of her more as an *it* than as a *her*. The female then becomes a possession for personal pleasure and self-indulgence.

All important: Self-indulgence leads to self-disgrace and ultimately to shame. Self-discipline leads to self-esteem.

LUST	LOVE
Sees sexual object as a thing.	Sees sexual partner as a person.
Asks the question: What would I like to do?	Asks the question: What is the right thing to do?
Is what makes you feel ashamed after it's over (*a long time after*).	Is what makes you feel clean in God's sight—after it's over.

WHAT IS LOVE?

> LOVE IS MY DECIDING
> TO MAKE YOUR PROBLEM
> MY PROBLEM——AS
> LONG AS YOU ARE ALIVE!

The fulfillment of lust always leaves us with a violation of our self-esteem. For this reason, it is very common to find cases of men who have murdered their mistresses, or women who have murdered men whom they sought in lust. After awhile, the exercise of lust so destroys man's self-love that one is tempted to redeem his self-love by liquidating the stimulating object of his lust, which has brought the shame and disgrace to his own self-image.

Is sexual relationship outside the bond of marriage moral or immoral? It is immoral because it tends to generate shame instead of esteem. Love involves trust, faith, and respect. If, therefore, the sex drive is based on genuine love, then there will be the respect for the partner, and the faith and trust in the partner, which will naturally invite marriage. If two young people want to have sexual relations but do not want marriage,

> it must mean they do not want to assume responsibilities, which means they choose privileges without responsibilities (a self-disgracing, self-esteem-lowering principle);

> or it may mean that they do not respect each other enough to commit themselves to spending the rest of their lives in an act of comforting, strengthening and supporting each other. (That's what marriage is!)

I was asked by an interviewer on television recently, "Don't you think that if two young people wait until marriage to experiment with sexual relations that they may find that they are incompatible?" The answer is obvious, *Ridiculous!*

The truth is that sexual compatibility is not something that happens naturally. It is an art that is developed in a matter of many months and years. As a pastor, I have counseled many husbands and wives who had been married for a few years and still had not achieved sexual compatibility, but through competent counseling by their doctor they achieved success in this area. Obviously, they could never have achieved (or tested) their compatibility through sexual relations prior to their marriage. Even more, the sex act is so sensitive to the emotions of both partners that the test of compatibility must be made in an atmosphere where fear, guilt, and other negative emotions are totally absent. This is seldom possible in premarital sexual relations. For that reason, not a few teen-agers have engaged in sexual relations without real fulfillment. They never married because they concluded they were sexually incompatible. The truth is they might have been sexually compatible if they had been free to experiment over a period of months and years, in a guiltless, shameless, fearless environment such as is provided under the marriage arrangement.

Since sex is such a vital part of life, it is imperative that we begin our sexual history in such a way that it will start without a memory that is tinged with any fear, shame or guilt. To all of the teen-agers who are reading this book, I would say: Be smart! Let your wedding night be your first sexual experience. To the girls, this will mean that your sexual experience will have with it no fear of rejection. There will be no anxiety that he might dump you in a week or a month. Sex is meant to be enjoyed, and you cannot enjoy it fully and completely if it is tinged with guilt, shame, remorse, or the worry of exposure, rejection, or pregnancy.

Meanwhile, marriage will have a greater possibility of lasting success if it begins with an unforgettable, positive, emotional launching. To participate in premarital sex will deprive you of the one organic-generating, emotional experience of unforgettable intensity— nature's way of launching marriage with a traumatic christening. To have premarital sex is like nibbling through the day. By the time the banquet hour arrives, you have spoiled your appetite; or if you have not spoiled your appetite, you have lost the joy of anticipation. Don't deprive yourself of the joy of deferred gratification. I promise you this: On your wedding night, if you have waited until you are married, you will both be proud of yourselves. This untarnished self-love will make possible the enjoyment of sex to its fullest potential.

5. DON'T LET YOUR SELF-LOVE GO TO POT

The "high road" does not lead to happiness. Narcotics do not build self-esteem, rather they serve as an escape from facing up to yourself. Remember, you will never be happy until you are able to live with yourself and enjoy yourself. The high feeling that comes through narcotics is a counterfeit self-love. Authentic self-respect comes when you know you are building a constructive life for yourself and for others. Happiness is in helping people, not in escaping from reality.

6. PLAN YOUR LIFE AND WORK YOUR PLAN

Pick a goal and strive to reach it. Aim to arrive at your goal by the age of forty. Too many young people wait until they are forty before they decide what they want to do. It is easy to assume in your teens that you have a whole lifetime to do something worthwhile. If you wait until you are forty, you only diminish the possibilities of your fulfillment and increase the obstacles immensely. It's still possible to build a great life for yourself after forty, but strive to have your base well laid before you reach your middle years.

Don't fall for the eat-drink-and-be-merry-for-tomorrow-we-die philosophy. I recently counseled a young person—an eighteen-year-old boy, who was all mixed up. When I asked him why he went out and got drunk he answered glibly, "Well, who knows, I may have to go to war and die. Or the atom bombs may fall around me and we may all be blown to smithereens. I don't know how long I am going to live, so I am just going to enjoy it."

I answered, "My advice to you is: study, work and be serious, for tomorrow you may live! You may not die in war. There may never be an atomic war. Tomorrow you may live! And you will regret your wasting of these years. Study, work, buckle down and if you are alive tomorrow, you will be thankful to God that you sowed fruitful seed. This is the road that leads to a wonderful sense of self-worth."

7. SUCCESS IS WHAT YOU ARE, NOT WHAT YOU DO

For a philosophy of success and failure, remember this: You can achieve what you can believe. In the final analysis, however, your greatness will be measured, not by what you have done, but by what you have become. Build a great character and a great reputation as a wonderful person, and you will be a success!

The most treasured freedom that you have is the freedom to choose your God. Choose your God! After that your God will determine your person, and your destiny.

8. SPEAK YOUR PIECE ABOUT PEACE

On the whole subject of war and peace, never forget that war is almost always the destruction of human life and the demolition of human dignity. But do not fall for the false line that war is always wrong. When America went to war to help abolish the Nazi regime in Germany, war was essential. Horrible as hell though it was, its aim and purpose was the liberation of human beings and salvation of human dignity.

Peace without freedom leaves no room for self-respect. Peace without justice, without freedom, without the opportunity for every man to speak his mind, is inhuman and worse than death.

9. REMEMBER THAT CONFORMITY IS NOT THE WAY TO REAL POPULARITY

Every teen-ager is in the phase of life where he seeks to develop his personality, discover his own identity, and become aware of his own selfhood. This is never accomplished through mass conformity. Nobody else is just like you are. To find out what you are, you must stand on your own two feet.

Don't be a follower. Be a positive-thinking young leader. Check and correct some of the negative thoughts that are making the rounds in the youth culture today.

NEGATIVE THOUGHTS

THE OLDER GENERATION MESSED UP OUR WORLD. True, they have made mistakes, but think positively. What have they accomplished? Polio wiped out! Anesthesia, antibiotics, and aspirin tablets! Eye transplants, kidney transplants, and heart transplants! Because of the older generation, every young person born today has a chance to live twenty years longer and is healthier than those born a century ago.

THE ESTABLISHMENT IS HYPOCRITICAL. Of course! Hypocrisy will always be present in a sinful human race. But wait a minute. What is hypocrisy? Is it failing to live up to a standard we profess to believe in? No—or every person would be a hypocrite, except for Jesus Christ. Hypocrisy is failing to live up to your own standards, but trying all the time to give people the impression that you are!

What is hypocrisy? Jesus answered that. He said: "And why quibble about the speck in someone else's eye—his little fault—when a board is in your own? How can you think of saying to him, 'Brother, let me help you get rid of that speck in your eye,' when you can't see past the board in yours? Hypocrite! First get rid of the board, and then perhaps you can see well enough to deal with his speck!" (Luke 6:42 LB).

Young people, before you criticize your older generation for their faults, make sure your generation is faultless. First clean up the sins such as widespread drug abuse and irresponsible breeding of children. In one twelve-month period, there were forty-five thousand illegitimate births in California alone! At this rate, America will be turned into huge fatherless communes, creating more ghettos—pockets of poverty and crime. The great American Negro, the Rev. Dr. Leon Sullivan, has pointed out that the black problem in America stemmed from the lack of the father figure in black society. It started in slavery times when the man was sold, leaving his woman. A whole black culture evolved with women and illegitimate children. The problem this produced is a matter of record.

10. FOLLOW THE GLEAM OF GOD'S DREAM FOR YOUR LIFE

The fact that you are alive enough to read this paragraph is proof of the fact that God has a plan for your life. If you are an atheist, I have news for you. You may not believe in God, you may deny God, but you can never stop God from loving you. He lives. He loves you. And there is not a thing you can do about that. He has a dream for your life, even if you don't believe it. He has a plan for your life, even if you don't discover it.

You will achieve real self-love when you discover that life is worth living. Life is worth living when you find a God who is worth serving.

Christ is a God worth serving. Let Jesus Christ come into your life and you will really begin to live.

Don't be afraid of it. When Christ comes into your life, He doesn't kill you. It is true that some things die when Christ comes into our lives. Worry over the future dies. Fear dies. Hate dies. Guilt dies. Boredom dies. Inferiority complexes die. Resentments die. When they die, you start living!

A young teen-age girl handed me this essay, entitled "Me, Myself and I."

Why was ―――― born? What is she in search of? Where is she going and why? I want to be quite frank and honest with you; I have nothing to hide. Why did God put me on this earth? What is His great and wonderful plan for me and my life? Again, I don't know. We just have to live each day to the fullest and believe in Him. Many people are apprehensive about the future. I am not —not in the least. What can worrying do—that believing can't? The most important part of my life is my religion. I don't mean to sound like a religious fanatic because I am not—but since Jesus Christ came into my life I have become a positive thinker. There is nothing like thinking positive.

Many things are impossible with man, but nothing is impossible with God. It is easier to be happy with thinking positive. In the morning I get up and thank God for the good night's sleep I have had and ask Him to guide me in the coming day. All of the decisions are left up to Him, in other words I never make a decision without consulting Him about it. For example, last summer I had a chance to go to Guatemala with a few other young people. I really planned on it. I prayed about it. The next night I walked into my room quite late and saw a spider on the wall. It must have taken me twenty minutes to get enough courage to kill that darn thing and another fifteen minutes to clean the mess off the wall. I got to thinking that if it took me that long to kill it at home what would I ever do in Central America, because I am sure they are much bigger there. So I began to believe that God was telling me that I should not go to Guatemala. The next morning I received an unexpected call with a job opportunity that I have accepted. And it is working just great. With God on my side I don't have anything to worry about. I live by the words of Christ, "If you have faith as a grain of mustard seed you can say to this mountain, 'Move . . .' and nothing will be impossible to you" (Matthew 17:20).

An enormous sense of self-love comes into your life when Jesus Christ comes into your life. A beautiful young girl from our community went up to Berkeley, California, where she began dropping acid. Marijuana and LSD became a way of life for her. When her parents telephoned her to come home, she agreed with only one objective—to tell her father and mother that she was going to go back to Berkeley and never come home again. I received a telephone call from the parents who urged me to talk with her while she was spending the weekend at home here. They came into my office together, father, mother, and daughter. She was a mess! Her beautiful young face was distorted from her inner tensions, guilt, and hardened attitude. Very sincerely she declared to me, "I have found God in LSD. Every Friday night we have our services. It's beautiful! You don't know what God is like until you've found God in LSD."

"I believe I have found God in Jesus Christ," I replied. "You claim," I continued, "that you have found God in LSD. Who's right, you or I? Let's put our gods to the test," I suggested. "God is love—agree?" She nodded her head approvingly. "Love is helping people," I added. "Agree?" She nodded her head in agreement. "How much money have you collected in your LSD services," I asked, "money to feed the hungry, to help crippled children, to find a cure for cancer?" She was silent.

"I must tell you," I went on, "because of the Spirit of Jesus Christ that lives in the lives of people in this church we have given over $50,000 in the past twelve months to help human beings with problems. The Christian church has built hospitals, institutions for the blind, the sick, the lame, and in foreign countries for lepers."

The sad look of disillusionment began to creep over the face of this young lady.

"Let's all stand, hold hands, and pray," I offered. The father, mother, daughter, and I joined hands in a circle. We offered this simple prayer: "Jesus Christ,

Your spirit of love lives within my heart. I pray that You will come into the life and heart of Mary Jones." When I finished I saw a tear slide out of her eye, and roll down her cheek. My finger reached over her soft cheek, picking up the wet drop of warm emotion. Holding it before her I exclaimed, "Mary! Look what fell out of your eye! Didn't you feel beautiful inside when this tear was forming and falling? This is the deepest and most joyous experience a human being can know. It is religious emotion. It is the movement of a divine Spirit within you. Christ is coming into your life! Let Him come in. Don't be afraid of it. Nothing good ever dies inside when Christ comes in. Many wonderful things come alive inside of you when Christ comes to live in you. Look at the sky—it's blue. Look at the grass—it's really green. Look at the flowers—they are really red. While you had this high trip which put this beautiful tear in your eye, you were in complete control of yourself. This is reality. It is not an artificially induced stimulus. It is authentic. The world around you has not been distorted or hidden in a psychedelic fog. You can trust this Christ." At that point tears flowed freely out of her eyes. Jesus Christ took control over her.

Immediately, her facial features changed. The narrowing eyes of suspicion and rebellion changed into the round, open, beautiful eyes of a wonder-struck girl. The face which was formerly tight, tense, and almost old looking, suddenly relaxed. Once more the cheeks had the full blossom, the warm rounded shape of a pretty young maiden. Today this lovely girl is devoting her life to helping young people discover that the greatest trip you can take is when you tune in to Jesus Christ who really turns life on, for when Christ comes into your life you cannot hate yourself. You can only love yourself when He is a part of you.

6

THE PARENTS

Six Success Pointers for Parents

To succeed as parents has never been more challenging than it is today! Young people are bright and alert today.

The Sunday-school teacher was clicking nicely. She asked the class, "What do we learn from the story of Jonah?"

Replied one eight-year-old modernist, "Travel by air."

I am sure we'll all agree it is more difficult raising children in today's world, though it has never been easy.

Children now live in luxury, they have bad manners, contempt for authority; they show disrespect for elders and love to chatter in place of exercise. Children are now tyrants of the household. They no longer rise when an elder enters the room and they contradict their parents. They chatter before company and gobble up the food at the table, they cross their legs and tyrannize their teachers.

Socrates produced those thoughts two thousand years ago.

Not long ago, I flew by special invitation to be with a friend of mine, Billy Graham, at an Eastern Crusade. A great crowd was already gathering, beginning to fill a thirty-five-thousand-seat auditorium, when I arrived. For me, one of the unforgettable moments of my life came a half-hour before the service began. I was led backstage, through a rear door, to a house trailer. My guide knocked three times. The door opened and there stood Billy Graham, smiling, waiting for me. "Come in, Bob, how nice of you to come," he said warmly. We sat alone and talked and shared and prayed. Then it happened! His children came in, Franklin and Bunnie. Suddenly a little fellow, probably three years old, came tearing up the trailer steps, rushing among all of us to the open arms and beaming face of Dr. Billy Graham. "Grampa! Grampa! Grampa!" the little boy shouted. I shall long remember that lovely scene as Billy proudly introduced me. "My grandson," he said. The joys of success as parents are priceless.

If I am communicating now to a young couple starting on the threshold of marriage, I say: The joys of parenthood are priceless!

I like that story that Daniel Behrman, the Jewish humorist, told. He was illustrating Jewish humor in Israel. The story concerns a cabinet meeting where the

Israeli Government was looking for a way out of the country's economic difficulties.

One of the more obscure counselors suddenly jumped to his feet. "I've got it! I've got it! We'll declare war on the U.S.!"

"War on the U.S.? Are you *m'shuggeh?*" (My Yiddish spelling is purely phonetic.)

"No. It'll be over in a couple of days. Then they'll come and occupy us. They'll rebuild the country. They'll give us new factories. They'll make us a Marshall Plan! We can't lose!"

The whole cabinet concurred excitedly with the exception of one man. Rumor says it was Dayan. He merely asked, "What if we win?"

"What if we win?" Before I give you the price of parenthood, let me give you the rewards of victory. They are pride, joy, love—all the days of your life!

The rewards are worth all of the risk, the work, the sacrifice, the anxiety, and the tears that go into the long (and yet so short), the difficult (and yet so beautiful), the trying (and yet so touching) task of raising children in today's world.

Six Success Pointers for Parents

1. Be Assured Parents

Be confident that you can succeed! By all means believe in your ability to succeed as parents. A young wife and husband were sterilized before marriage, because, as the wife stated to me, "I'm afraid to raise children in today's world."

An excellent book on the subject was written by Marguerite and Willard Beecher, titled *Parents on the Run*. The authors see fathers and mothers running scared. It's understandable, of course, if you look at the dangers, temptations, and sins in today's youth culture, but a great deal of anxiety is the result of confusion in counsel offered to parents.

The authors of *Parents on the Run* rightly point out that modern parents have been the victims of a sad kind of education that has led them to believe they dare not trust their good horse sense in matters relating to the rearing of their children. The closing sentences of the book are beautiful. "Remember that as the tree inclines so was the twig bent. Live on a self-sufficient, self-fulfilling, and productive basis yourself, and your children will live likewise. Then you will enjoy them. They will enjoy you."

You can be assured that if your marriage is happy, then the soil is right for successful parenthood.

A couple were having their weekly fight concerning their families.

"You never say anything nice about my family," the wife complained.

"Yes, I do," her husband countered. "I think your mother-in-law is a lot nicer than mine."

Build a strong and happy marriage and be assured you can succeed as parents, too. There will be many times when you'll wonder. Take assurance from God's promise:

Teach a child in the right path and when he grows up he will appreciate it. (Proverbs 22:6)

A newspaper article titled "My Father" presents it well.

When I was 7, I thought—My father is the smartest person in the world. He knows everything.

At 17—My father doesn't know as much as I thought he did.

At 21—My father doesn't know anything, compared to me.

At 35—My father knew much more than I thought he did.

At 50—My father was always right.

Let me share with you the Parents' Creed which I wrote for Mrs. Schuller and myself.

The Parents' Creed

I believe, that my children are a gift of God— the hope of a new tomorrow.

I believe, that immeasurable possibilities lie slumbering in each son and daughter.

I believe, that God has planned a perfect plan for their future, and that His love shall always surround them; and so

I believe, that they shall grow up!—first creeping, then toddling, then standing, stretching sky-

ward for a decade and a half—until they reach full stature—a man and a woman!

I believe, that they can and will be molded and shaped between infancy and adulthood—as a tree is shaped by the gardener, and the clay vessel in the potter's hand, or the shoreline of the sea under the watery hand of the mighty waves; by home and church; by school and street, through sights and sounds and the touch of my hand on their hand and Christ's spirit on their heart! So,

I believe, that they shall mature as only people can—through laughter and tears, through trial and error, by reward and punishment, through affection and discipline, until they stretch their wings and leave their nest to fly!

Oh, God—I believe in my children. Help me so to live that they may always believe in me— and so in Thee.

2. Be an Attentive Parent

Children seek and need attention. If they don't get it from you, they'll get it elsewhere. What they really want is guidance in the evolving process of self-discovery.

The teen-ager's struggle to identify himself was reflected in many of the two thousand entries of boys and girls, thirteen to nineteen years of age, in the annual creative arts competition of *Youth,* a magazine for young people of the United Church of Christ, the

Protestant Episcopal Church, the Church of the Brethren, and the Anglican Church of Canada. Award winner Pat Werkman expressed it in "The Cry of the Teens."

> I am here,
>> but I don't know where I am
> I know where I came from,
>> but I don't know where I'm going.
> I know my name,
>> but I don't know who I am.
> I'm living the "happiest days of my life,"
>> and I'm crying.

Listen when you hear them. Join them when you are with them.

Look upon your child's request, "Read to me," or "Tell me a story," *not* as an *interruption* but as the most *honored invitation* you'll ever receive. It is an invitation to shape an immortal soul!

3. Be an Available Parent

Simply be there when they need you. Two extremes must be avoided.

Overpossessiveness. Here the parents control the child, restricting the free development of a unique individual. Never try to force your child to fit into the imaginative box you have cut out for him.

Overpermissiveness. Here the parents fail to shape, mold, and form the character of the child. Discipline is nonexistent. The life becomes a river without banks—and that always turns out to be a swamp.

Simply be available to your children. Ask questions. Attend their school functions. Answer their questions. Be available to take them to church. Busy? Months ahead of time, mark their functions on your calendar.

4. Be Affectionate

Say it!
Show it!
Share it!

Love is still the divine word. Love your child as someone who needs you desperately. Imagine that this child is *you* with the calendar rolled back many years. Put yourself in this child's shoes, then respond in love. Love your child. What more can be said? Demonstrate unconditional, nonjudgmental love. Now, and always.

5. Be an Authoritative Parent

Perhaps the best book on this subject is Dr. James Dobson's book titled *Dare to Discipline*.

During the early days of the progressive education movement one enthusiastic theorist decided to take down the chain-link fence that

surrounded the nursery school yard. He thought
the children would feel more freedom of movement without that visible barrier surrounding
them. When the fence was removed, however, the
boys and girls huddled near the center of the
play yard. Not only did they not wander away,
but they didn't ever venture to the edge of the
grounds.

Discipline defiance out of your children. Every or-
ganization needs authoritative leadership, or anarchy
will result. Children will, from time to time, test and
challenge your role as authoritative leader. When that
happens you must not—you cannot, you dare not—
lose. You must be the authoritative leader of the
family.

Defiance must be punished. Spare the rod and spoil
the child. Cultivate the art of spanking. Here are some
rules to follow:

(1) Always spank when the child is openly defiant.
(2) Be sure the child is warned beforehand: "Obey.
     If you don't, you will be asking me to spank
     you."
(3) Spank very hard—but very carefully. Never
     bruise, or injure your child's body. Use the
     flat of the hand (on the soft behind). Never
     strike the head.
(4) Make the spankings rare and memorable occa-
     sions. If you spank for every little childish act,
     it will mean nothing.

(5) Explain carefully that you are doing this because you love him and your love compels you to teach him that serious misdeeds are painfully punished in the school of life.

(6) Welcome him into your arms when he cries with a penitent heart.

(7) Pray lovingly and affectionately with him as you embrace him after the whole spanking is over.

(8) Expect the usual results. Both parent and child will be drawn closer together in the whole episode.

(9) Be honest. Be frank to tell him that you, as a parent, are imperfect. You make mistakes, too, and you suffer because of this, too. By this honesty you cease to be a hypocrite in his eyes. Such sincerity will win his respect.

6. *Be an Aspiring Parent*

Discipline them. Now, dedicate them.

Roots and Wings

Give them food,
Give them clothes—
These are needful
Heaven knows.
Give them bikes
And cowboy boots,
But first of all
Give them roots.

Be their guide.
You won't be always
At their side.
With all these things,
But don't forget—
Give them wings.
Let them soar.
Let them see life
An open door.
You may skip
Some other things—
But give them roots
And give them wings!

BETTY S. BURNETTE

One of the most helpful pieces of advice I ever received was from the principal of the junior high school. The first of our five children was entering junior high. The principal was speaking to parents: "Give your children goals. The junior high students who have goals stay out of trouble. Don't worry that you'll be forcing your unfulfilled personal ambitions upon your child. Remember your child can change his goals in high school and college. But they must have goals through these junior high years!" So Mrs. Schuller and I followed that advice and really gave this assignment Number One priority.

Give your child an inspiring example. I know many parents who have given up smoking and social drinking in order to be the most inspiring examples to their children. It's been proved that no youngster tries drugs without first trying a cigarette. "My parents drink cocktails to relax. Why can't I use marijuana or pills?" a youngster argues. The argument may or may not be valid. Nevertheless, pull the rug from under the argument. Quit smoking and quit drinking! Suddenly, your child will learn from your inspiring example the lesson of how to give up his own bad habits.

Now, give them a faith to live by. God *is* alive, whether you believe it or not! Find God yourself. Search for Him. Buy a modern translation of the Bible. Read it. Look for a happy church. Turn to Christ. Find out what He believed about God, faith, prayer, and eternal life. Follow His faith and you'll be in the Best Company. Now, share this with your children. It's still true!

The family that prays together—stays together.

7

THE HOMEMAKERS

Homemakers: God Bless You!

In the final analysis, success in marriage and family will depend to a large extent on the homemaker. I attribute my family success largely to my wife, Arvella Schuller, a successful homemaker. Here is a transcript of a message she delivered in the church on Mother's Day. For your last lesson on happy family living, listen to her advice. She's a winner!

I don't believe there is any group of people today that needs God's blessing more than the twentieth-century American homemakers. Here in America, the homemaker feels that her career is unfulfilling, unattractive, and outdated. She feels she needs to play a more important role in society—that it takes very little brains to run a home. In fact, being a housewife is not only obsolete, it is just downright stupid.

So homemakers are flocking to the business world to demand equal status with man, seeking fulfillment and respect in society. Meanwhile, it has been reported in the press that in Russia, Khrushchev announced after World War II that all able-bodied women would be released for full employment and that day-care centers would be established to care for the children. The Kremlin has abandoned the goal of building day-care centers because there is now a steady increase of Soviet wives, whose husbands have sufficient income, staying home. The government newspaper published an article calling for a redefinition and upgrading of the social position of a homemaker. A government correspondent even proposed that a mother who stays at home to care for a family should be entitled to a government pension for the significant contribution she makes to society.

Let's take a new look at homemaking in America. We need to think of homemaking as a much broader and larger career than most homemakers themselves realize. We underestimate all the roles and jobs. It is true that we are already liberated housewives. The push-button age has liberated us from a great deal of hard work. Automatic washers and dryers, dishwashers, the add-water-only cake mixes, the TV dinners and just-heat-and-serve foods, no-clean ovens—all are liberating us from much of the hard work of homemaking. But as the physical part of being a homemaker shrinks with pushing buttons, so the role of the home manager is more complicated and significant. It takes a lot of brains and know-how to be an efficient home manager.

Let's look at some of the roles under the umbrella of home manager. This is as complicated as managing a small business. My role as a home manager for our household of seven includes being a good time-manager. To keep five children organized on five different school schedules is no small item. Add to that piano-lesson schedules, doctor and dentist appointments, church and choir schedules, and my husband's schedule, and then the organizing and scheduling of my time to fit into their schedules.

As a home manager, I must be sure that the physical needs of my family are met through proper rest, exercise, food, and vitamins and minerals. I need to be knowledgeable as a dietician and food expert.

In our home, I act as chief purchasing agent. While big businesses provide intensive training for their buyers, I must, with very little training, make the necessary purchases in food, clothing, appliances, and household articles. I have to know where and how I can make the best purchase.

Since we have children, I need to have a great deal of knowledge about child psychology and behavior patterns. I need to be a child expert.

Under my umbrella as home manager, I am the bookkeeper—stretching the household budget to include that extra item we didn't count on

—and treasurer. (My husband is the corporation president. Wouldn't you know! He gets two votes to my one.)

Then there is the role of filing expert. With the large amounts of mail that come into our home, I must sort, process and file the necessary papers. There are the warranties of the shaver, the mixer, the vacuum, the camera, the electric curlers—with instruction sheets of what to do in case. There are all the records for income tax, Social Security, Blue Cross, car insurance, house insurance, loan agreements—each with small print to be deciphered. (That reminds me: I never did read the small print on our marriage contract.)

Add to all of these roles, the roles of chauffeur, maid, referee of sibling rivalry, nurse, wife, mother, queen!

If we take an open and honest look at homemaking, *it is an immense career more complicated and complex than most wives admit and husbands understand,* and ours is a constantly changing role in a changing world.

There is a theory that by the year 2000, small computer consoles connected with central station complexes will help with family budgeting, tax calculations, school work, purchasing and menu planning, library and reference sources, mail order and shopping services. The family's newspapers, magazines and books may be brought to the home by teleprinter.

There will be automated kitchens. The homemaker may make out her menu for the week ahead, put the necessary foods in the storage spaces and give instructions to her kitchen computer. At the prescribed time, mechanical arms will get out the preselected food, cook it, and serve it.

Homemakers will go to the store by videophone. Many wives may have a robot maid that is trained to the requirements of a particular home and programmed to do specific tasks.

A multiarm robot will wash windows, sweep floors, vacuum rugs, dust furniture, clean windows, brew coffee, and pick up your husband's clothing.

There will even be antigrouch pills for those who are mentally healthy, but chronically irritable. Some argue that personality drugs should be available to the public, so that husbands will always be ambitious, wives always understanding, children always well behaved!

The twentieth-century American homemaker has problems in her career because she does not have the proper respect and understanding for this complex career. Furthermore, the homemaker has difficulty because she enters her career so inadequately prepared and trained for it.

Mothers take great pride in giving their daughters the best in dancing, music and the arts, and this is good. But mothers must also prepare their daughters in the art of being effective home-

makers, training them in the creative and positive aspects of the home.

Dr. Samuel Kling, a divorce lawyer and author
of *The Complete Guide to Divorce,* claims that
"inadequate preparation is a major reason for
divorce and breaking up of homes. We train for
everything but marriage. Marriage may fail simply because intelligent preparation is lacking. It
takes a lot of training to become an accomplished
artist or musician. What would happen if the
Establishment would require marriage courses in
the first year of high school? We spend nothing
on education for marriage and the making of a
home."

The two semesters of home economics for girls
and biological sex studies are the only preparation that I know of in our school. As a result, too
many couples rush to the altar completely un-
educated and completely unprepared for marriage and the art of making a home. What would
happen if our schools could include such courses
as *How to Choose a Mate; Differences in Male
and Female Personalities; The Function of a
Home; The Importance of the Home to Individual, to Community, and to Country?*

I say that the career of the homemaker is
an *immense* one, and, in order to succeed as a
homemaker we need to think of homemaking as
an *imaginative* career—a career which requires

a great deal of creative thinking and acting. Women, by nature, are creators. Motherhood begins with the highest experience known to the human being—taking part of creating a human being in the image of God!

One reason housewives are disillusioned with homemaking is that the automatic age has squelched much of the creativity.

For example, I remember how Mom Schuller's eyes would glow as she brought out her apple pie —the most delicious apple pie I have ever had. It was her creation! She picked the apples from the tree in the backyard and then she would proceed to create her pie. Much of this kind of creativity has disappeared in our twentieth-century-instant-serve home life. Homemakers need to be challenged to direct all their creative imagination and ability to make the home and the family a strong institution again. A home is something more than just four walls—more than a place where a group of people eat and sleep together.

Home is a place where a family learns together and where life's most important lessons are taught. Smiley Blanton, an eminent psychiatrist, says, "Eighty percent of the problem patients that have come to me, came because good manners were never taught to them as children. As adults, they made mistakes and were rejected. They couldn't play the game of life because they didn't know the rules."

Home is a place where the family grows together. A college student, in tribute to her mother, wrote: "Thank you for growing beside me, and always ahead of me."

Home is a place where the family lives together. Sometimes we are at our worst—other times at our best. Robert Frost said, "Home is where—when you get there they have to let you in." Someone else said, "Home is where we grumble the most—are treated the best." Home is where the great are small and the small are great!

As homemakers, we need to use our creative, God-given imagination to ask, "What are the needs of my family? What is the real function of our home? For our family, in our busy life, I know that *our home has to be an oasis* where we can be filled up again, and refreshed for the hustle and bustle of life.

For this reason, we have one of our unique rules: No rock and roll music. We find it adds too much noise and tension, and destroys the atmosphere of calm and quiet.

I admire the creative and independent thinking of a judge's wife who refuses to have a television. It is an interruption, and adds confusion to the home. Because she will not have it, she feels that the children have learned to be much more creative in their everyday living.

Dare to be different! Dare to be creative!

Another function that requires imagination as a homemaker is the creation of happy memories for the family. Sigmund Freud pointed out that what we describe as character is based on the memory traces of our earliest youth.

What are some of your nicest memories of childhood? Most likely they are the simple things that you remember. For that reason, we make a big thing out of family celebrations. The birthday candle that won't blow out has already become a tradition in our home. The children can't wait to find out which candle on the cake will keep glowing.

Mrs. Neutra, widow of the late Richard Neutra, just last week spoke enthusiastically about memories of her childhood. "My luck was to grow up in the atmosphere of a happy marriage, with three younger sisters and wonderful memories of birthdays and Christmas celebrations. My mother had a marvelous gift for making such events memorable. She would, for instance, on the spur of the moment decide to cook an especially good dinner, set the table festively, dress us in our best dresses, and put on her best evening dress. My father donned his tuxedo and we would celebrate being a happy family. All the girls would display their talents—playing the piano, singing, reciting a poem—and my father would make a speech."

Mrs. Neutra concluded, "These memories

make me believe that the foundations of one's own character are not only the genes which you inherit, but the example of your parents and the congenial atmosphere you grow up in."

A young wife, whose husband became unemployed, was asked how she managed to remain so cheerful and positive. She said, "Because I have a memory of my mother's 'trouble meals.' My mother would scrimp and save to make an extra-special, nice meal. (This was during the depression.) She did this to show our family that she believed in her husband and in his ability to fight back."

My husband and I both grew up in homes where the family devotions took place after the meal was over. We have adopted this method for our home, even beginning devotions while the smaller children finish their dessert.

During World War II, one of my brothers was in the South Pacific in the navy, and another brother was in Europe. More than once, they wrote back saying that they received new courage just knowing that the family was praying together each night—holding hands. They had a memory of being part of that circle and this now gave them the courage they needed.

The little ones in our family already are having their memories molded by the prayers they recite. Their favorite from Sunday school is one of gratitude.

Thank you for our happy hearts,
For sun and rainy weather.
Thank you for the food we eat,
And that we are together. *Amen.*

One woman recently told how she found a way to relieve tension simply through the memory of her mother. When things became difficult and tense, the mother would drop her work, go to the bedroom, and close the door. Sometime later, she would open the door and come out a completely different person—peaceful, calm, and happy. One day the woman's curiosity caused her quietly to open the bedroom door. She saw her mother on her knees at the side of the bed, receiving strength and power through prayer. This woman, through the memory of her mother's therapy, has discovered this same power available to her.

The career of homemaking is an *immense* career, an *imaginative* career and a *most important* career! My theme as a mother and homemaker is simply this.

Some men build bridges—
Others plan skyscrapers,
But a mother molds leaders for tomorrow.

"An eagle stirreth up her nest so that her young may fly," is a Bible verse I use in my experience of preparing our children for the time when they will be adults. I have a keen sense of awareness of this responsibility. It is important for me as a mother to know that my children are not really my own, but a gift—a trust from God.

> We give Thee but Thine own,
> Whate'er that gift may be.
> All that we have is Thine alone,
> A trust, O Lord, from Thee.

Our children are a trust from God—to mold, to teach, to lead so that tomorrow there will be voices of love, positive faith, inspiration and encouragement to fill the vacuums of the masses.

When a boy or girl thrusts his small hand in yours, it may be smeared with chocolate ice cream, or grimy from petting a dog, and there may be a wart under the right thumb, or a bandage around the little finger, but the most important thing about the hands is that they are the hands of the future. These are the hands that someday may hold a Bible or a revolver; play a piano or spin a gambling wheel; gently dress a bleeding wound, or tremble, wretchedly uncontrolled by a drug-addicted mind.

Right now that hand is in yours. It asks for help and guidance. It represents a full-fledged mini-personality to be respected as a separate individual whose day-to-day growth into adulthood is your responsibility.

THE SUNDAY SCHOOL UNION

Most of us as homemakers and mothers feel inadequate in our position. We don't know how to cope with messy children, dirty clothes, disorganized schedules, houses so automatic they automatically break down. Then, too, we have idealistic memories of the perfect mother we had, and unrealistic goals for ourselves. Add to that the awesome responsibility of knowing that if we don't do our job, our children will grow up to be dropouts, and failures for the future.

How can you and I be successful homemakers?

Here are five suggestions that work for me as a homemaker.

1. We Must Be Possibility Thinkers

It is most important that we develop positive mental attitudes. It is not so much what we *do* as what we *are!* We develop a positive mental attitude by surrounding ourselves with positive-thinking people and projects. The books we read, the television we watch, the music we listen to, the friends we have—all have a powerful influence on our mental thought patterns. We must make sure they are *positive* influences on us!

2. We Must Define and Understand Our Roles

For me, my husband is first; my children are second; my career as a pastor's wife, with its many responsibilities, is third.

Two women, friends of mine, are top executives in the business world. Many men would be honored to hold their positions. Even these successful career women are quick to say that their husbands are first, their families are second, and their careers are third. They are very successful in marriage, in the home and in their careers.

3. We Must Live Our Faith

A letter came this week from a teacher of the Now Generation. She has had nothing to do with organized religion since she was a child. In trying to find a television program for her child, she came across "Hour of Power," and her letter read:

I am slowly beginning to feel that those pupils I have taught, who believe in God, are more constructive in their approach to life. Somewhere along the way, these children must have been exposed to people who acted morally. It all began with their parents. When I meet these parents *who live by their beliefs each day,* I can see why their children respect them.

4. What Place Does Jesus Christ Have in the Home?

For our home, we have adopted the theme

Jesus Christ is the Head of our house;
An unseen guest at every meal;
A silent listener to every conversation.

It does make a difference! I don't know how I can teach the children some of the most basic values in life—without God.

When our family was smaller, we had an extra chair at our table, and it was just understood that Christ was there on that chair, with us.

5. *Is Christ the King of My Life?*

It is self-centeredness that causes the problems in our working world and in our personal relations. It is self-centered living that is the damaging force within the home. The only way that I can conquer self-centeredness and become others-centered is through becoming Christ-centered. I asked Him to take over my life as a young girl and He is the One who makes the difference.

Someone has to be King! Put your hand in the hand of the Man who calmed the water. When He is King, He is there, available to help you through any situation. When the storms come, the foundation of your home will remain solid and strong.

My husband received this letter from a mother:

I am the mother of two girls, one eighteen and the other sixteen. This past summer my eighteen-year-old was graduated from high school with music honors. She worked this last summer to save money for college. Come September, she came to her father and me and said, "I'm leaving home. I'm going with some girls and boys to live in a commune." You can imagine what a shock it was to us. Nothing we said to her made any difference. She said she had to find out what she really wanted. My husband and I both ended up under doctor's care. A girl who had never been away from home, who always had whatever she needed! Three weeks went by, and we never heard a word from her. Then one night she called, "Mom, I'm sorry I haven't written but we've been living in the mountains and it's so hard to get a ride into town. This girl and I hitchhiked to call. I've been sick with dysentery from the water here. We are leaving now. We're on our way to San Francisco. Please don't worry about me. I love you and Daddy. I'm so mixed up. I'll find what I really want soon." Well, you can imagine how I felt.

The next day I was in the hospital. They say it was tension and nerves. One Sunday I turned the TV on and your program came on—"Hour of Power." I'd never heard of it so I left it on. When you came on, it was as if you were speaking just to me. You said something about faith and letting Jesus Christ guide you. Something came over me. From that Sunday on I put my daughter's hand in Jesus' hand and I let Him take care of her. Every morning I knelt down by my bed and I said, "Jesus, I'll put my hand in yours, you take care of all my troubles."

Six weeks ago my daughter called me and said, "Mom, can I come home?" I never thought I'd hear those words. She had been working in a hospital in San Francisco and she said that's what she wanted to be, a real nurse. She came home, she's in nurse's training, and loves it.

I know that Jesus brought her home to me. He took care of her. He had her by the hand, just like He had me by the hand.

Walk with Christ in a glorious career here on earth and through eternity!